TIME FOR TEA

Time for Tea

Tea and Conversation with
Thirteen English Women

TEXT AND PHOTOGRAPHS BY
MICHELE RIVERS

Portrait photographs by Arabella Ashley

Crown Publishers, Inc. / New York

Published by Crown Publishers, Inc., 201 East 50th Street, New York, New York 10022. Member of the Crown Publishing Group.

Random House, Inc. New York, Toronto, London, Sydney, Auckland
http://www.randomhouse.com/

CROWN and colophon are trademarks of Crown Publishers, Inc.

Printed in Hong Kong

Design by Nancy Kenmore

Library of Congress Cataloging-in-Publication Data
Rivers, Michele.
 Time for tea : tea and conversation with thirteen English women / by Michele Rivers.—1st ed.
1. Tea—England—Social aspects. 2. Women—England. 3. Drinking customs—England.
4. England—Social life and customs—20th century. I. Title.
GT2907.G7R58   1994   394.1'5—dc20   93-42375

ISBN 0-517-59219-3

10 9 8 7 6 5

For Two Precious Beloveds
Tom Bowlin
and
Danielle Elizabeth—my girl

CONTENTS

VIRGINIA,
LADY BATH
MARCHIONESS
OF BATH
. 79 .

Age 75   Widow
Mother and Grandmother
Artist
Lady Bath's Gift Shop

ELIZABETH
BROOKS
. 91 .

Age 33   Divorced
Mother
Executive Assistant,
D. J. Miles Co.,
Tea Blenders

LADY JANE
BOLES
. 99 .

Age 57   Divorced
Mother
and Grandmother
Owner, Country
Boarding Kennel

FRANCES
EDWARDS
. 109 .

Age 49   Married
Mother
Owner, Edwards Bears

EMMA
MAITLAND-
WALKER
and
HELEN
STONEHAM
. 117 .

Ages 15
Students

ACKNOWLEDGEMENTS

*A*CKNOWLEDGING THOSE WHO HAVE HELPED AND ASSIST-ed me in the creation of *Time for Tea* is such a privilege. Thank-yous, hugs and much love to all of the following: Arabella Ashley—Ari's thirteen portraits are wonderful. Going on location with Ari and her dog Clem is always a wild adventure. She's a brilliant photographer and good chum. My family, for all their collective help and boundless support. An extra big kiss to my mother, Mary, for teaching me, at such an early age, the art of making a delicious Sunday afternoon tea. Dear Di—Dianne Rasmussen and her artist's eye on location. Sue Larsen, a great cook—testing recipes in a Larsen-built kitchen is a dream. The Four Fers—Mike, BJ and Becky—such wonderful supporters. Massive thanks to Laurie Harper, my agent, Jane Cavolina, my editor and Kim Hertlein, my production editor—all Anglophiles through and through. And finally, love and thanks to all my dear tea-sipping friends—Mari, Carole, Fred, Kaoru, Mary Brent, Linda, Nancy, Jongie-Lisa, David, Karen, Alice, Nick, Monica, Ingrid, The "Outback Crew", Sue, Gillian, Lindy, Mandy, Ian, John, Ros, Doris, Tim, Franz, Leslie Michael, Danielle and Tom Bowlin—who have all shared not only endless pots of tea with me over the years but their hearts, hopes, fears and dreams; these are the friendships of a lifetime, of soul and of inspiration.

Dear Friend,

The initial idea for *Time for Tea* evolved during an afternoon tea party with some American friends, while drinking endless cups of tea and munching on far too many cucumber sandwiches. Although I am completely guilty of keeping the English afternoon tea myth well and truly alive, I found myself trying to explain that tea for English women is not often in the formal style. That the elegant afternoon teas portrayed romantically in old films—tables draped with finest Irish linen, Aynsley teacups, crustless sandwiches, a stately silver teapot and Dame Peggy Ashcroft presiding over the whole affair—are completely different from the way most English women enjoy their tea today. My teas do include the trimmings, right down to the infamous silver teapot, and I even keep a secret stash of rich yellow clotted cream tucked away in the freezer, ready to defrost at a moment's notice! However, in *Time for Tea* thirteen English women from vastly different backgrounds, with varied lifestyles and of different ages, will show you the variety of ways we English women enjoy our tea. Tea nurtures the soul and revives the spirit, so I recommend that you put the kettle on, make yourself a pot of tea, use a cup and saucer instead of a mug, kick off your shoes and cuddle up in your favourite chair with *Time for Tea* and enjoy your "cuppa" with some new friends.

Fondly,

Michele

THE ONE-AND-A-HALF-MILE TRACK TO GREENALEIGH FARM IS really only suitable for horses, Land Rovers and sturdy walking boots. This lone farmhouse sits on the Somerset coastline; just one small field separates the beach from the cluster of farm buildings and the house. It's a magnificent sun-filled location in late spring and summer but wickedly grey, cold and desolate in winter. This is where the Slade family lives. Anne and Paul, with their four children Nichola, Ben, Oliver and Sam, share their home with a vast menagerie of pets: Flash, the faithful golden retriever; the three cats, Gobolino, Rupert and Outdoors; a horse, numerous sheep and various Gloucester Old Spot pigs. The kitchen is the nucleus of this home. Fully equipped with all modern conveniences, it somehow manages to retain an easygoing farmhouse charm. A beautiful antique foot-pedal organ rests against a stone wall, away from the working end of the room. As soon as the kettle sings, Anne warms the teapot with some boiling water, sets it to one side as she mutters something about how important it is to always warm the pot, then digs about in a cupboard for the tea caddy and the biscuit tin. After the teapot is sufficiently warmed Anne empties it, mentions her dislike for tea bags, spoons three heaped teaspoons of black tea into the dark, glossy brown teapot, fills it up from the kettle and joins me for tea and conversation at the kitchen table.

"I drink coffee by the gallon, but at four o'clock I always have a cup of tea. I would never drink coffee then. I'll make myself a pot of tea because it's teatime and I'll sit down and really enjoy my tea."

THE CHILDREN TOLD ME THAT THEY DON'T HAVE strong feelings about the tradition of tea, and my initial thoughts were similar. But when I sat down and thought about it more, I discovered that tea has a much more important part in my life than I realized. I now wonder if I feel the way I do because I was so tied to this tradition of always having afternoon tea as a child. Tea was such an important part of our day.

The coastal path to Greenaleigh Farm.

It's not the same for my children. My children just say, "Tea is sitting in front of the television on Sunday afternoons with piles of hot buttered toast." We only have afternoon tea on Sundays because we have a big Sunday lunch at one o'clock. What time you eat your main meal makes a difference, doesn't it? We have our tea while watching *Songs of Praise* on the television. This is so different from the teas my brother and I had as children. Perhaps English tea traditions will die with my generation.

I drink coffee by the gallon, but at four o'clock I always have a cup of tea. I would never drink coffee then. I'll make myself a pot of tea because it's teatime and I'll sit down and drink my tea. When I've got coffee I drink it on the go, when I have tea I sit down and really enjoy it. It's interesting, an inbred sort of thing even though it's just a cup of tea. I always use a cup and saucer and I can't bear tea bags.

Mother made tea for us every day after school, then we had dinner with my father when he came home, which was quite late. I think afternoon tea is basically a class thing. It goes back to the aristocracy having their formal tea around four o'clock and then eating dinner later. Working-class people just didn't

have the time or the money for all of that. Our lifestyles are completely different today too; few people have the time for preparing two meals after work.

We drink Indian tea mainly, it's a very strong breakfast tea blend. Usually we have sandwiches at our Sunday tea. The traditional sandwich for me is Marmite and watercress. We've just started growing our own watercress. We have a spring that comes out of the hillside so there's constant running water, which watercress thrives on. You can just go outside, pick it and make the sandwiches. We sometimes make up a batch of sandwiches with jam and cream which are delicious. Occasionally we have honey on bread and butter and sometimes a cake that Paul or one of the children makes. It is a simple recipe: six ounces of flour, four ounces of butter and two eggs—I can remember 6–4–2. Set the oven for 350 degrees and the cake will be done in about twenty to twenty-five minutes. It's what I've always made, what my mother taught me.

Teatime treats galore.

One of my childhood memories of afternoon tea involves our holidays in Kent. I had three aunts and two grandparents who all lived in the same town and when we went to stay there, each one wanted to give us tea. We would spend our afternoons going from house to house having tea, one after the other. It was absolutely dreadful! We couldn't say, "No, thank you, we've already had tea," because they would be most upset. There would be crabapple jelly and homemade cakes and you just had to sit down and eat it all. It was particularly difficult at my grandmother's. You couldn't possibly say you weren't hungry there, and Gran always had simply masses to eat! It was a family joke en route to Kent to say, "Get ready, it's the four teas again."

Tea was always with the family: aunts, grandparents and the children on Sundays. It's accepted in England as just tea, it's not thought of as anything special, usually, just tea. I suppose it's what you're used to. My brother goes out to tea every Sunday throughout the year. He takes the whole family, that's his tradition. Perhaps the English tea shop is the only formal way people have tea today. For me, my childhood memories are afternoon tea and ballet lessons, that's it, in a nutshell.

I had a career as a ballet dancer and then I taught ballet. After that I got involved in voluntary work and somewhere during all this we had four children and for years I was at home with them. Later I worked part-time in a probation department and this got me thinking, "Why not go the whole hog and do a law degree?" Now four years later I'm still amazed that I've done it. I'm sitting here grinning because I'm proud of myself. I decided to do it and I've actually done it! I'm still suffering from shock, I just finished the last exam!

This whole midlife career change came about because of a conversation I had with my friend Rose. For some unknown reason we decided that at thirty-five we only had ten good years left. God only knows why we decided that forty-five was the end of our lives! It wasn't funny at the time, we were quite depressed about it. If I remember correctly, we drowned our sorrows in several pots of tea and ate a whole packet of biscuits. But age doesn't seem to matter anymore. Now I'm thirty-nine I still think I've got ten good years left and hopefully I will think the same way when I'm forty-nine. Anyhow Rosie started marathon running and I decided to go back to school to get the qualifications I needed to start studying for a law degree. I really didn't think I could do it, I had to practically start from scratch with my education. It was Paul, my husband, who encouraged me.

It was difficult at school in several ways; my first classes were with sixteen-year-olds. When the teacher called out the morning register it was rather embarrassing: "Caroline, James, David, Sara, Sam and . . . Mrs. Slade." I remember cringing at that. Some teachers found it equally hard having an adult in the class as I did. Thank heavens my children weren't at the school then. I remember when we had breaks, the students would go off to the six-form block [the student room] and listen to music, the teachers would go to the staff room and I would end up sitting in the classroom all on my own with my mug of tea. I was unsure of myself and I didn't quite know how or where to fit in.

Now, after four years as a student I wouldn't hesitate to join in. It was a case of lack of confidence. Since then I've changed totally, absolutely and utterly. I've grown up! It sounds ludicrous at thirty-nine to say I've grown up but I have. Actually setting a challenge and completing it has given me masses of confidence. I was confident before I had the children. While I was at home my confidence seemed to disappear without me even realizing it. For years I didn't meet anybody. I got out of the habit of actually talking. I think that made a huge difference, not having day-to-day contact with anyone other than the children and Paul. I wasn't unhappy at home but I was very scared going back into the world again.

All our lives have changed since this decision four years ago. Paul has been absolutely and utterly supportive, and unless you have a husband who is supportive you can't do it. There's no way I could have done it on my own, because when I'm away Paul's got to take

Which path to take? . . . Follow your heart.

over with the children and when I think I'm going to fail he tells me, "Of course you're not going to fail." He encourages me whenever I need it. Next year I've got to go full-time at a law office; it's going to be difficult, to say the least. The whole family is adjusting. We explain to the children what's going on and basically just talking about it solves most of the problems.

Redirection can often be difficult, but our family has managed well. I know several couples in my year at law school who haven't coped with the adjustments. I think it has something to do with the men not adjusting to the change in the women. It's interesting watching the female students alter over the years; cutting their hair, losing weight, using nicer makeup and wearing smarter clothes. One particular friend at school is unrecognizable from the person who came in the classroom on the first day. It's extraordinary to watch the metamorphosis. The changes are far more evident in the female students.

Achieving what I set out to achieve is about the most important thing to me. I wanted four children and God willing I've got four healthy children. I wanted a law degree and I've got a law degree. It's the actual *doing it* that counts. Words mean nothing without the action. It's a challenge being at law school and it's always a challenge being a parent. We really enjoy our children and we've always insisted that the children don't do what they're told just because they've been told what to do. We want them to think first, then do what they're told because we've given them a good enough reason. As they get older that means they very often change our minds.

I'm totally female and yet I never wear anything but trousers! I'm a contradiction! I wear perfume every day, Opium because it's expensive and I happen to like it very much. I'm at a very bad place in my life where I'm confused about being female. I can't really define what being a female means to me. On one side, women have the best bit of the bargain, we can have children, which I think is brilliant. That must be the best experience of my life, having our children. Yet sometimes I feel I have the rough end of the bargain and I wish I wasn't a woman. I'm just about to leave being a full-time mother. I feel total guilt, absolutely, totally. I don't feel that I should be at home ironing shirts for school, nothing like that. I showed all the children where the iron was many years ago. It's just the idea that I won't be around so much. I think a lot of career women feel guilt. I don't see how you can exclude the guilt aspect, particularly if you have four children. If you want to give them decent parenting it means you've got to give them emotional time. There's no way you can do full-time work outside of the house and be there every time they need you, so you're going to have emotional conflict constantly. That's no new statement—every working mother must feel this way, it just so happens that I'm coming fresh to it at the moment. Paul does more than fifty percent of the parenting already. He's going to reduce his time spent at the medical practise to part-time, so it will be Dad running the house.

It's exciting to have all these changes in our lives. But the truth is . . . on Monday I'll be excited, on Tuesday I'll be depressed, on Wednesday I'll be guilty, on Thursday I'm going to shoot myself and on Friday I'll be really enthusiastic again! In six months I may be another person, I'm not sure who!

Paul and the children explode into the room, shattering the momentary sadness that hangs in the air. Comments about the day's school activities, homework, starvation and rugby practise fly around, as Anne's face changes from that of contemplativeness to the enthusiastic mum, delighted to be a part of all the after-school activity. The remaining teatime biscuits vanish before our eyes as one by one, four ravenous children join us at the kitchen table. "Hey Mum, any more tea left in the pot?"

ANNE'S BUTTER SHORTBREAD
. . .

"I thought this recipe would be tasty and easy. Be warned you can never eat just one piece of shortbread, it's extremely moreish. In England we often make shortbread at Christmastime. It's delicious with a glass of sherry too!"

Anne Slade

1 cup/250 g best-quality butter
½ cup/100 g white sugar plus extra for sprinkling

2 cups/250 g all-purpose flour, sifted, plus extra for flouring

Preheat your oven to 350° F/175° C.

In a medium-sized bowl, cream the butter and sugar together with a wooden spoon, or use a mixer. Gradually work in the flour with your hands until you have a smooth, binding consistency. On a lightly floured surface, knead well to a smooth dough and roll out to ½ inch/ 1 cm thick. Cut the dough into fingers or use a biscuit cutter—any shape you care for—or press into a shortbread mould.

Place on baking tray and prick the top of the shortbreads with a fork. Bake 15 to 20 minutes, until very pale golden and the bottoms are slightly brown. Leave for 1 minute to cool, then transfer to a wire rack and sprinkle well with extra sugar while still warm. When cool, store in an airtight container.

Makes 24 biscuits

SUGGESTED TEAS: My favourite—loose Indian black tea or try Keemun black tea considered by many connoiseurs to be one of the finest Chinese teas. A caffeine-free Egyptian chamomile would be good too.

ROSE TANNER

*G*ATEWAYS IS A SMALL SUPERMARKET NESTLED IN THE HIGH STREET between the butcher's and a specialty wine shop, situated in a typical English country town. In June, July and August the town is filled with tourists from the northern industrial counties, and you'll overhear farmers' wives complaining about the parking problems. Their weekly shopping excursions to town in winter are far less time-consuming, by all accounts. They all, however, enjoy the increase in their farmhouse bed-and-breakfast business and the occasional Indian or Chinese meal, in restaurants that exist solely due to the influx of summer visitors. I had done my fair share of mental grumbling regarding parking problems when a car pulled out of a highly prized parking spot in the center of town. A quick dash into Gateways would have me back home in plenty of time to get dinner ready. Queuing at the checkout counter with my tomato puree, I overheard the cashier talking to the woman ahead of me. "Hello dear, is this all today? Oh, do I need my afternoon break, I can't wait for a cup of tea." This thirsty lady was Rose Tanner. We got chatting about tea breaks and before the next customer was served we had made an arrangement to share a flask of tea in the staff canteen the following week. Looking very smart in her freshly laundered Gateways uniform on the appointed day, Rose settled in her regular spot at the Formica table in the staff room. She unpacked her carrier

"In a crisis we English often say, 'Come on, sit down and have a cup of tea and we'll talk about it.' I can't tell you how often in my life I've heard those words."

The rose-covered garden fence.

bag; sandwiches and biscuits appeared. Then she poured her steaming tea from a sparkling white thermos.

The other employees soon took their breaks and we finally relocated to the only available place with any privacy: the fuse room! Here we sat face-to-face in semidarkness on a couple of cases of toothpaste, knees touching in a room barely big enough for an electrician let alone two women and a thermos of tea!

I FIND MY JOB BORING AND YET FAIRLY STRESSFUL and hectic at times. I'm under a lot of pressure when we're really busy. When I do get a break it's great to just switch off with what I class as my lifeline, my tea. From a very early age tea was a mainstay in our home both in good times and in times of stress or unhappiness. It's very English, to put the kettle on and talk things out, over the great British cup of tea.

For the English, tea is an icebreaker. You can develop a friendship with somebody over a cup of tea, you know, like we use the subject of the weather to help make conversation. The first thing you hear when visiting someone's home is "Would you like a cup of tea? I'll put the kettle on." Tea is a big equalizer. It doesn't have to be anything fancy. Most people drink your common old general make, I do. If I feel like spoiling myself I'll get out the Earl Grey, that's my treat. If I'm in a hurry I just pop a tea bag into a mug, but if I'm sitting down to really relax then I make a nice big pot with loose tea.

Now that I'm single, I don't make teatime eats much. When I was married I baked regularly: fruitcakes, lots of scones, biscuits, plain fare but the kind of food that goes well with a cuppa. A nice piece of fruitcake in the one hand and a cup and saucer in the other . . . is a perfect combination.

I've got a great memory of one very special cup of tea. Through the last stages of labour with my first child, when I got to the point of no return, I thought, "I can't handle this anymore." I remember a lovely little nurse saying to me, "Not long now dear, and as soon as it's over, we're going to bring you the best cup of tea of your life!" After the birth of my beautiful daughter, they propped me up in bed and sure enough the nurse brought me this cup of tea. I can recall it most clearly. It was the best! It *was* terrific!

Having the experience of being a mother for the first time was wonderful. It was the highlight of my life. It's really an exciting thing to be a woman and become a mother, sharing everything about yourself, all your feelings, all your love with this growing person. Some people view children as a liability or things to be picked up and loved when it's convenient. I think it's one of the greatest privileges in the world to be blessed with the care of, the nurturing of another human being.

I've made some good friends since moving here. I love the area, the country town, the scenery that's all about us. I originally came from Swindon, which is described as one of the fastest-growing towns in Europe. People have moved in from the Greater London area and it's changed the place, it's fast-paced, it's got an impersonal feel to it. I find living down here the pace is generally slower. People have roots here and care about one another, it's a true community.

Buttercup making the morning "pinta."

I was a bit concerned that it might be hard making friends but people seem to notice others more in country towns, especially newcomers. My neighbours introduced themselves straightaway. I was up to my ears in piles of moving boxes when one neighbour popped her head over the garden fence and said, "I've put the kettle on. Would you like to come over, put your feet up for ten minutes and we'll introduce ourselves over a cup of tea?" We've been friends ever since.

My life has been quite a battle really. I've been married twice. I married my first husband at nineteen and had a child more or less straightaway. I have two lovely daughters. But life was very difficult emotionally and financially from the word go. It was a bad marriage, inasmuch as we were both very insecure and very young and we didn't have the support around us that we needed. Although we stayed married for nineteen years, in the end it got very nasty and painful. Things became quite violent and abusive, I couldn't tolerate that type of behaviour anymore and I filed for divorce. Leaving was a huge step for me to take. I was quite frightened of being alone, but for the next seven years I was. I got a good job, my own little home, my independence. I was set and I thought, "Finally I've made it."

During my first marriage, I took escape in alcohol. I continued my drinking after the divorce. After being single for years, I met and fell in love with another chap, and we decided to take the plunge and get married. What I didn't realize was that I had gone straight back to the same type of man I had married before. I've always prided myself on being fairly intelligent and perceptive, but emotionally I've got lots to learn. I knew that if I was going to overcome the kind of problems we were faced with in the marriage, I'd have to do it as a sober Rose. The booze had to go! I'd hidden behind it too long.

Finally, I decided to make myself a healthier person so I could attract healthy people to me. My daughters and I had long talks, it took quite a bit of healing time for them. Now we've got a good relationship. I'm looking forward to having grandchildren. It would be lovely to regain some of those lost years with their children. I'm on my own again and feel very positive about the future. I plan to make more friends and attract relationships which are good for me.

I'm really proud that I managed to stop drinking. I've learnt to love myself, with warts and all! Now I know there are alternatives. I can solve a problem in a more positive way. Writing poetry is a wonderful outlet for me, I can write for hours, I pour my heart into it.

Ready for the milkman.

A host of golden daffodils.

Life has got a lot to offer, I lost so much of mine and now I want to make up for all those lost years. Funnily enough, sometimes people have to go through a lot of unhappiness and pain before they become who they really are.

I believe we're here for a specific reason, wherever we're born or whatever circumstances we're born into. Women have got so much going for them although our talents aren't always recognized. I think we are our own destiny; through who we are and what we pass on to our children, we create and mould the future. That's why I want to travel. How exciting it would be to go to different parts of the world and discover how other people feel about their lives, and how they view others across the continents and oceans. To really see the world, meet new people and find out why they do what they do, what makes them tick. I think all too often in life we are fearful, afraid to do lots of things, but we'd be really pleased if we took that initial first step. Chatting with someone, you often find out that they've done something, accomplished something, and hearing that gives you courage and incentive to get cracking.

My goal is to be open to all I see, never going through life with blinkers on. Keeping both eyes widely open and welcoming what's new and sometimes a bit frightening. You don't have to have great big goals in life, even the smallest thing can be a most important step sometimes. Often at the end of the tunnel you can walk out of the fog into brilliant sunshine.

In a crisis we English often say, "Come on, sit down and have a cup of tea and we'll talk about it." I can't tell you how often in my life I've heard those words. It's funny to think that tea could be so important to me, but it has been a real comfort in my life. Brits use tea as a way to show we care. The making of tea—the kettle for boiling water, the teapot and the brewing time— perhaps it's a sort of therapy, giving a person something to do, feeling useful in a crisis. As I said, a cup of tea has often been my lifeline.

ROSE'S LEMON CURD
. . .

"Lemon curd is very English so I thought I'd give you this very simple recipe. Lemon curd makes a lovely gift to a friend. It doesn't keep very long and needs to be refrigerated. You can use it as a filling for a Victoria sandwich, fill tarts with it, spread it on bread and butter or toast. You can put it on scones I suppose, but you don't really see people doing that in England."

Rose Tanner

Note

Giving Lemon Curd away as gifts? Try covering the top of the jar with a circle of yellow gingham fabric and tying with raffia.

*3 lemons, 4 if small
2 cups / 400 g sugar*

*6 large eggs, free-range if possible
½ cup / 125 g butter*

Carefully grate the rind from the lemons, removing the yellow zest but none of the white pith. Squeeze out the juice. In a small bowl, mix the rind and juice with the sugar. Beat the eggs well. In a double boiler, melt the butter and add the eggs and the sugar mixture. Cook over medium heat, stirring constantly, until the mixture is very thick and coats the back of a wooden spoon. Spoon into sterilized jars, cover, label and refrigerate.

Makes three 12-ounce / 375-ml jars

SUGGESTED TEAS: An iced herbal lemon tea would be nice, especially in the summertime. In winter try my favourite treat—Earl Grey. It has a lovely amber colour and can be served either with lemon or with milk.

INDON FARM'S KITCHEN IS SPACIOUS AND FULL OF LIFE. FISH swim in a tank on the corner cupboard, three cats jockey for position in their basket by the oven and dogs stroll through to antagonize the cats or to check if food has appeared

"I love my horses, my husband and my children, but not necessarily in that order. I hate big spiders found unexpectedly, injustice, being overweight, and last but not least, sugar in my tea."

in their bowls. Children's swimming costumes hang over the radiator to dry, a kettle steams away on the stove and a lump of dough cooking in the bread-making machine fills the kitchen with a yeasty aroma. Jugs of fresh milk sit on the counter ready to be decanted into nipple-topped bottles for feeding lambs. The phone rings and a bed-and-breakfast guest can be seen climbing over the piles of mud-clad Wellies at the back door. Moments later Penny Webber comes running into the kitchen, kicking boots out of her way. After she promises to make lunches for the guests'

outing, takes a booking on the phone, sorts through a stack of post, drolls momentarily over the outfit on the cover of a fashion catalogue, detangles daughter Emily's hair, forces vitamins down David (her son's throat), yells something to a painter up a ladder outside . . . Penny pulls up a chair and joins me for a mug of tea at the kitchen table.

OH, THIS TEA IS NECTAR! A CUP OF TEA IS JUST THE job. Some days you just need one desperately, on a day like today, for instance! I've had a hell of a morning. This local tea from Porlock is awfully good. We aren't big on herbal teas in this house. There's a couple of boxes of peppermint and lemon somewhere—the mint's good if you have an upset tummy.

We're not cups-and-saucers here on the farm unless it's a special occasion, there's too much going on for all of that. I grab a mug of tea and often end up drinking half of it out in the stable with Fleck, my mare, or up at the barn, even in the poultry run. Very rarely do I enjoy a full mug of tea while it's still hot in the mornings. We always have tea first thing in the day before we cook breakfast for the guests. If Roger, my husband, knows I'm having a hard time getting going in the morning then he brings me up a mug. On birthdays it's tea and breakfast in bed.

Our guests love the farm, they often join in with the activities and there's always something going on around here. Princess Gloria, our Gloucester Old Spot pig, farrowed last week, she did well, thirteen piglets. We lost one. I gave it mouth-to-mouth resuscitation and palpitated its heart but it just wouldn't come around. Heaven knows what I could have caught, I dread to think! Gloucesters are pink with black splotches and the piglets look like slimy little sausages when they come out. It only takes them a minute or two after birth to climb around and latch on to mum's teats. It's an incredible sight to watch.

A couple of weeks ago my mare had a foal, that's a big event on the farm. The filly's gorgeous, we named her Model Image—Midge for short. How those long legs fit inside the mare, I don't know. It's marvelous! I'm a nervous wreck when Fleck is in labour, so much can go wrong with horses. She lost her first foal and I was depressed for weeks after that. So far so good with this one, touch wood. As I say,

Gloucester Old Spot piglets.

32

Chrysanthemum, the family cow, with Hindon Farm in the background.

there's always something going on at Hindon: ducklings, chicks, budgies, rabbits, goats, dogs, cats, turkeys, sheep—you name it, we've got it. Oh yes, and Huggy our donkey. Huggy's extremely friendly and quite safe for smaller children to ride. It's no wonder he's so fat, our guests all give him carrots! Most of our visitors come from towns so their children have masses of fun playing farmer: collecting eggs, feeding the chickens and exploring acres and acres of land.

Having a successful bed-and-breakfast business is a lot of hard work. It cuts into our family life quite a bit, but it really is one of my proudest accomplishments—that and having two children. When we took over this farm, it was in pretty rough shape. We completely redecorated it from top to toe. Rog took out the tile fireplace in the sitting room. My father designed and built an Adam-style surround and we installed that to replace the awful tile thing. We sanded, stained and varnished the dining room floor, slapped on gallons of paint all over the place, papered, plastered, carpeted and generally ripped our

way through it all. Hindon's not one of these overly decorated places mind you, it's still very much a farm. Friends say it has a very comfortable feeling. I used either Laura Ashley fabrics or wallpapers in most of the rooms and the local house sales and auctions provided affordable furniture and paintings. In less than six months we practically had the whole place and the guest wing redecorated.

The middle section of the house, which includes the kitchen, is actually the oldest part of the farm and dates from the late sixteenth century. The rest was added in the eighteenth century. Hindon Farm is recorded in the Domesday Book, which means there's been a working farm on this land since 1066! Roger's family has lived here for three generations. Our children, David and Emily, could be the fourth generation of Webbers to work this farm but with how farming is going in this country they may not get a chance. It's hard to make a decent living in agriculture these days. That's why so many farms are forced into taking guests to survive. Diversification is the key to country survival today. I hate to see lovely old farms sold off or split up but it's happening all over the country. People just can't make ends meet. Fortunately, I keep very booked up with guests. We have the best of both worlds here, isolated in our own valley yet close to town.

One of my favourite things to do is to have tea with my female friends. Occasionally after collecting our children from school we might congregate at one of our homes. We have a cup of tea and a gooey cake from the bakery. I had an elaborate tea party a couple of weeks ago. Friends came to stay from America and my sister Susan and her children were visiting, so we all had a huge English tea. It was rather on the spur of the moment, so I did my favourite thing, picked up the phone and ordered all the baked goodies from a fabulous little restaurant: scones, ginger cake, a jam sponge, shortbread biscuits, raisin loaf, even a Victoria sandwich. I jumped in Morris, drove to town, picked up my order, bought a pot of cream and a few other incidentals and managed to whiz home to make sandwiches before anyone arrived. The table was absolutely overflowing, tea for the

Opposite: "One of my favourite things to do is to have tea with my female friends." From left: Gregory, Susan, Angie, Penny (with teacup) and Christine.

starving masses in minutes! Everything is homemade from the restaurant, it's awfully extravagant of me but a girl's got to do what a girl's got to do.

Morris is my car, a cream-colored 1960 Morris Minor convertible. Driving with the top down and Tina Turner blaring out of the tape deck is my idea of bliss. Going forty miles an hour is zooming in Morris. It's that way with old cars—they rattle and shake and you feel like you're flying along. Having this illusion saves on petrol and speeding tickets! Morris is just like me, dumpy and dangerous!

Practically all of our guests visit Selworthy village, which is just over the hill. Periwinkle Cottage is a lovely place to have afternoon tea, and it's right on the village green. I send them dozens of customers every year. Sometimes I take a friend there or go with my sisters for a cream tea. We walk up over the farm, down the lane, past the church and there you are. The views are lovely on the walk. I don't think the exercise quite wears off the effects of the cream tea, mind you, but it helps. Periwinkle's a beautiful cottage, with a fabulous fragrance inside. It's a sort of mixture of gorgeous baking and English lavender furniture polish. On chilly days they get a fire going. It's smashing to walk in on a cold Sunday afternoon, pink-cheeked from the wind and chilled to the bone. The tea warms you right through and you feel . . . oh, I don't know quite how to put it . . . I suppose safe and protected from the elements really, sitting by the fire sipping tea and munching on scones. It fortifies you for the walk home! Of course they make their tea in the real English way, warming the pot with boiling water before putting in the loose tea. God forbid a tea bag would ever cross their threshold. The scones are served warm with jam and clotted cream—oh, I can taste them now, they're simply out of this world!

I don't make tea treats like I used to. I'll occasionally make Mum's fruitcake or a bakewell tart, but nowhere near as often as I did. I do so much cooking for guests and our family meals, it has really taken the fun out of it for me. Unfortunately, I just have to look at food to put on weight so there's another reason not to make goodies. I also have a small business doing outside catering, so preparing food is too much like hard work these days. Rog likes to cook; he's terrific at breakfasttime, he can fry up eggs and bacon in no time and you should try his Sunday lunch—Hindon roast lamb, parsnips, roast potatoes, peas, carrots, mint sauce and all the trimmings.

We have quite a bit of home produce—milk, eggs, our own lamb and pork. There's a good-sized vegetable garden too. It's a beauty, huge and surrounded by an old red brick wall. The wall

An old-fashioned farmhouse tea.

*Rog relaxing with Spanner.
"Hurry up and finish your tea
so we can go for a walk."*

protects the garden from deer and the bad weather and I think it helps to keep the ground warmer. We used to have a gardener but we can't afford that sort of luxury these days so Rog takes care of it now, on a smaller scale.

We're very fortunate to live here, we know that. Mind you, nothing is idyllic no matter what it looks like to the world. With animals and guests you have to get up early—around seven A.M. I lay the breakfast tables for the guests before I go to bed at night so that's one less thing to do in the morning and I can lie in for an extra ten minutes. Once I'm up, the poultry is fed. I usually get distracted by something or somebody en route—a guest wants to feed the chickens or asks me if it's okay to let Dinky, our pet sheep, eat my flowers! At this point, I dump the chicken's corn bucket and pelt around to the front garden to rescue my roses from the jaws of bloody Dinky! Sometimes, I really regret saving that lamb! He was another of my mouth-to-mouth resuscitation cases. As I say, waking up is sometimes a nightmare! I must admit, I'm very easily distracted but once I hear "Eggs are ready," it's back to the kitchen and feeding time for the humans.

Rog usually cooks the breakfast for the guests and I serve. It's a fairly large meal, there's a choice of prunes, grapefruit or cereal. Then we serve the cooked breakfast: fried eggs, grilled sausages, tomatoes, mushrooms, bacon and fried bread, followed by toast with marmalade or honey. We have a beehive in the orchard; Roger is the resident apiarist. Most of our guests have tea with breakfast, very few prefer coffee. Our standard large Hindon breakfast is what most people enjoy and usually they eat every scrap. My mother insists it's the air down here that makes you hungry. I'm not sure about that but we don't get much in the way of leftovers!

My schedule is quite simple. I do the normal old household chores Monday through Friday, cleaning, picking up, putting away, washing and ironing—the typical boring tasks. On Saturday we have a changeover in the guest wing. It's a fully equipped flat that sleeps four. It takes quite a bit of cleaning after a family has stayed but I have two women in to help with this Saturday morning work. We all work together as a massive cleaning machine, zooming around with dusters, polish and brooms. A laundry service picks up towels and the bed linen. I'd never do anything else but housework if I didn't have my support team. Things tend to calm down in the winter. We don't have paying guests from the end of October to March. As much as we enjoy the guests it's wonderful to have the house back to just the family. David and Emily really love it because they don't have to be quiet and they get the run of the place. Having guests in your home is wonderful but sometimes it's a nightmare; as always there's two sides to everything. It can be quite a challenge, but the additional income does provide us with a lot of things we couldn't afford otherwise.

Gardening, office work, mucking out the stables—I fit them in when I can. There's always something to do around here. Other than the poultry and my horses, I'm really too busy to work on the farm much, except at lambing and shearing time, then I'm one of the team. I help pack the wool. The lanolin from the wool makes your hands lovely and soft but it's filthy work, you get covered in sheep muck. I cook the huge lunches needed for the shearers. They work very hard and have massive appetites. Shearing is backbreaking work. The guys we have are from New Zealand. They're incredible! They can shear a sheep in just minutes! They work their way around the world, sort of on tour as a shearing team. They make masses of money, work hard and at night often drink beer till they drop!

I actually prefer working on the farm to being stuck in the house. Believe me, farming's more fun than doing housework. I have simple likes and dislikes really; I love my horses, my husband and my children, not necessarily in that order. I hate big spiders found unexpectedly, injustice, being overweight, males without gumption, wearing glasses, mint–chocolate chip ice cream, male chauvinist pigs, flick knives and, last but not least, sugar in tea!

The road home to Hindon.

PENNY WEBBER'S MUM'S FARMHOUSE CAKE

· · ·

"This farmhouse cake is really yummy. It's great served with sharp cheddar cheese and sliced apples. Of course, it's an English tradition to serve fruitcake with a glass of port or sherry in the late afternoon if you forgo tea. I suppose that decision pivots on if there's any more work to do! We do the port thing usually at Christmastime, that's a special treat. Did you know that fruitcake was originally called plum cake in England? Nobody seems to know why, it never had plums in it. I know you'll love Mum's recipe, it's not a heavy fruitcake like so many are. It's moist and hearty and fantastically scrumptious. Enjoy!"

Penny Webber

2½ cups / 310 g all-purpose flour
½ teaspoon / 2 g baking powder
½ teaspoon / 2 g cinnamon
¾ cup / 150 g light brown sugar
¾ cup / 180 g butter or margarine, cut into pieces
2 eggs plus enough milk to make ½ cup / 125 ml, beaten

½ cup / 70 g currants
½ cup / 70 g sultanas (seedless golden raisins)
½ cup / 70 g raisins
½ cup / 70 g mixed candied fruit peel
½ cup / 70 g glacé cherries
½ cup / 60 g chopped almonds or walnuts

Preheat your oven to 350° F / 175° C. Grease a 7-inch / 18-cm round cake pan and line with greaseproof paper. Sift into a medium-sized bowl the flour, baking powder and cinnamon. With a wooden spoon combine the brown sugar with the flour mixture. Add the butter and mix until it resembles bread crumbs. Add the egg and milk mixture and beat again. Add the fruits and nuts and mix well. Spoon into the cake pan and bake 1¼ to 1½ hours on the center shelf of the oven, until a skewer comes out clean. Allow to cool 10 minutes, then turn out onto a wire rack.

Makes one 7-inch/18-cm round fruitcake; serves 8 to 10

SUGGESTED TEAS: Serve with China black, Lapsang souchong or English Breakfast tea. China black has a mild flavour and is excellent for afternoon tea; serve with or without milk. Lapsang souchong is a bracing, robust, clear and bright tea. It tastes a little of woodsmoke and has a hearty aroma. It is grown in the Fujian province of China. Apparently it is a big no-no to serve this tea with milk; however, I really like it with milk or lemon. If you don't care for this distinctively flavoured tea, try an English Breakfast blend. Can't decide on the right tea? Try sitting down with a glass of port and before too long, perhaps you won't care! Either way Mum's fruitcake will be divine.

To help keep your cake moist, put a tray of water on the bottom shelf during cooking. You can also add 2 tablespoons/30ml brandy to the cake mixture for added flavour. Make two cakes: Tie a tartan ribbon around one, and give to a friend, an instant celebration and great reason to put the kettle on.

CHRISTINE TAYLOR

*MAGINE A PICTURE-PERFECT ENGLISH VILLAGE. THERE'S A village green covered with lush velvety grass and a wooden bench for the weary traveler to rest upon. A Gothic church on the hillside presides over the thatched cottages, their whitewashed walls nestled against a backdrop of emerald trees. Curled up in a wheelbarrow, fast asleep, is a large marmalade-coloured cat, and nestled in a blossom-filled garden is a cottage tea shop. This scene really does exist—in the tiny village of Selworthy, and the tea shop is called Periwinkle Cottage. Quite a large portion of Selworthy is owned and governed by the National Trust, a private charitable preservation agency. Chris Taylor and her husband Mike lease Periwinkle from the Trust and operate a thriving business from the center of the village green. Periwinkle Cottage is everything an English tea room should be, with a thatched roof, country garden, rose-decorated china, sparkling teapots, pink tablecloths, a hint of lavender furniture polish in the air and mouthwatering cream teas. While the ground floor of the cottage houses the business, the upstairs is the Taylors' summer residence. After a busy day of cooking, this is where Chris relaxes. Enveloped in the down-filled cotton chintz of a huge overstuffed armchair, she snuggles into her evening with an enthralling novel and the marmalade cat from the wheelbarrow.

"Having a sign up that says 'Best Tea Shop In England' does increase the trade, and being featured in magazines brings more people to the area. You have to keep up the standard and have happy customers, year after year."

THE YEAR BEFORE WE TOOK over the lease of Periwinkle, it was voted "Best Tea Rooms in England" by the Tea Council. Several of the villagers asked me if I felt intimidated by the award Periwinkle had received. I wasn't bothered by it, no, not at all. I knew I could do even better! I must confess I was a little nervous the first morning we opened. But once that first customer came through the door I was fine. I just said to myself, "Well, I've got a high standard too." Then I was okay.

I make all my own cakes. Very few places actually serve homemade items anymore, it's too time-consuming. Our customers really enjoy the scones, pastries, cakes and gateaux we serve here. Homemade items are extra special and people really seem to appreciate my cooking.

Periwinkle was originally two cottages. That's why there are two inglenooks. One of our waitresses, Susie, lived in this cottage when she was a child. It's only been a tea shop since 1977, but they have actually had tea served on the village green for decades. Mike found a book at the library, *Selworthy 1850–1857* by Marian S. Archer Thompson. It was very interesting. Marian tells the story of how the tea on the green tradition began:

On my birthday the old people had tea all together under the walnut tree on the Green. This tea was started quite by chance. I was in Mary Eames's cottage with my nurse a day or two before my sixth birthday, and told Mary I should be six on such a day, the twenty-first of May. Nanny Down was sitting there, and Mary Eames turned to her and said, "Then you and I will have a cup of tea together and keep Missy's birthday." I said, "Oh, you should all have tea together." The idea was quickly taken up, and when my mother found that a tea on the Green under the walnut tree was to be held on my birthday, she had a big cake made and sent it up with some tea and sugar. The old people always managed this tea: we were only invited guests. My birthday has never been so honoured since. The teas were kept up for a long time after we left, till, as Mary Eames said, there were none of the old people left to come to them.

This original tea-on-the-green story is lovely, we were laughing about it the other day. Mike said, "Mary Eames probably had about half a dozen people to her tea. Now we serve over five hundred customers at the weekends in high season." What a difference!

Periwinkle is a very busy tea shop and it will just get busier and busier as people come to know us. On a summer weekend we probably serve around three hundred cream teas. Each cream tea consists of two scones, a bowl of clotted cream, strawberry or loganberry jam and a pot of tea. That's quite a lot to eat as the scones are a good size. Sometimes I'm amazed by how much some little old ladies can eat. After a cream tea they often order a piece of cake or a meringue and we serve both with a huge dollop of clotted cream. They eat up every crumb.

A welcoming sign to the thirsty walker.

Like most tea shops we do morning coffee and light lunches. Basically, I'm in the kitchen all day. The first thing I do when I wake up at seven is switch on the oven. I start with the Danish pastries, making about sixteen of those. Then I do the cakes. I like everything very fresh so other than the fruitcakes, I don't bake much in advance.

I make batches of scones as we need them throughout the day. Something is always cooking in the oven!

My baking takes me a couple of hours, then I have the soups and salads and things to prepare for the lunches. I don't want any help with the cooking because a small business has to be consistent. I can cope with the workload and it's such a small kitchen, I don't think I could manage with anyone else in there.

Mike works in the tea shop greeting, seating and serving the customers. He's very good with people, he chats to everyone and makes them feel at home. I would really like to be out there with the public, I enjoy that part of the business more than the baking actually. You don't hear praise often as the cook. Perhaps I feel slightly jealous of Mike because he's at the forefront all the time. He gets to work with the people and he gets all the praise for the work I've done in the kitchen! I prefer to do my own cooking and know it's good, but that does keep me in the background.

It's not easy living and working with your husband. Mike's really patient, but I get uptight sometimes, I suppose because we spend so much time together. Outside of my kitchen I'm a really easygoing person. But somehow when Mike and I work together my personality changes. We go walking together in the evenings, so that's a good relaxer. There are times when I feel I need to get away and be on my own, but my husband is the type of person who would get a bit upset if I said, "I want to go for a walk by myself." It can be a bit restrictive at times.

When I can switch work off, I relax and unwind and become myself. Then I'm a good wife again. What makes a good wife? Somebody who meets her husband's demands, I suppose. I think that women *should* be equal, but I don't think we ever will be, not in my lifetime. I think the wife will always be looked upon as below the husband. I'm striving so hard to be equal but I just can't get there.

I'm an independent woman really, not the motherly type, I'm a career woman. I've never thought about having another child after

I had my daughter Wendy. I really enjoy my work, despite the pressures and the limitations.

Wendy's married with a daughter of her own now, and she's expecting a second child in a few months. I adore my little granddaughter, she's precious. They all live in Nottingham and I see them quite often. I also have two stepchildren; Mike's son is twenty, and Ulandie is eighteen. They were fairly young when we married, and were with us on weekends and holidays and during the summer months too. They had a new stepfather first, before I came on the scene, so I don't think it was too hard for the children to adjust. We've been married eleven years now.

I consider Periwinkle as a workplace, not a home. Our house in Butley is really our home. With the tea shop downstairs and the

Selworthy village with the church commanding a fabulous view from the hillside.

A cream tea—delicious!

living quarters upstairs, I would feel like we never got away if we lived here all the time. On our days off we go back to Butley, do the gardening, the odd jobs. I like to entertain and we have quite a busy social life there. I suppose in some ways we have two completely separate lives in our two homes. We work hard for the things we want, it's a huge additional expense having a second home but it's worth it. Small villages like Selworthy are delightful in many ways but it can be a bit difficult working and living in such a small place. It's a really tight-knit community here, and I'm quite a private person really, so it's nice to sometimes have a bit of privacy and breathing space in a larger town.

Having a sign up that says "Best Tea Shop In England" does increase the trade, and being featured in magazines brings more people to the area. But the proof is in the pudding. You have to keep up the standard and have happy customers, year after year. It's so beautiful here. In the summer we open the gardens and serve customers outside. We've got a lovely variety of shrubs and flowers in the garden and lots of birds. The starlings and sparrows wait for the moment when they can fly down unseen to steal crumbs away from the tables. It's amazing how tame the wild birds get. Serving tea in the garden is ideal for walkers with their dogs. It looks like Crufts—the dog show, out there, some Sundays. Fortunately they are usually well-behaved dogs. Every English tea room has to have a cat wandering about and ours really acts as if she owns the place. The customers love her, she wraps herself around their legs and before you know it, they give her a taste of cream. She's really spoilt.

Our season is from mid-March until the end of October. We open at ten in the morning and close around five o'clock in the afternoon. When we first came to Periwinkle we did consider opening in the winter on the weekends, but it's absolutely dead here then, it's just not financially viable. So wintertime is when all the repair work gets done; decorating, major gardening projects, and we also go away on our holidays, so it's a busy time for us.

Even though we are a tea room we do serve quite a bit of coffee in the mornings. Mike roasts and grinds our own coffee beans and we're selling it by the pound as well. Our coffee is very popular.

We had a funny situation one busy Saturday with a tea customer. This lady specifically ordered a pot of Darjeeling. Mike by accident put the ordinary blend in her teapot. Darjeeling has quite a distinctive taste, quite different from our regular tea. We were just about to correct the mistake when we overheard, "This tea is lovely!" We did nothing, what could we have done? Maybe she didn't want to point out our mistake or perhaps she thought it was Darjeeling, I don't know.

Our house tea is excellent, it's Miles tea from Porlock. It's a blend that goes well with everything we serve. The most popular item on the menu is the cream tea. All our clotted cream comes from the local dairy, the milkman brings it every morning. In the high season we use as many as five trays of cream a day. If someone says "tea" to me now, the first thing I think of is our traditional full cream tea. We have tourists visiting Selworthy from all over the world. A cream tea is a highlight to the afternoon for many holiday makers. It's a tradition in Somerset and Devon, so there's lots of busy dairy cows in the southwest.

I never had cream teas when I was a child. I came from a poor background. There were four children and my father had a low income. It was a treat to go to an aunt's or to a friend's for tea, we

The tranquility of the English countryside nurtures the soul.

never went to tea rooms. To have a cream cake on the weekend was a very rare treat. Our teas at home were just the basic bread-butter-and-jam type. Occasionally, Mum would make cakes, just simple rock cakes, that type of thing, but we had nothing special really. There was no sitting around the tea table chatting and eating cream scones. Thinking about it now, I didn't talk to my mum much as a child. My father used to get us up and ready for school because Mum had to leave very early for work. She worked at night too so I only saw her for about an hour a day. I hardly got to talk to her at all. She was fairly reserved. I'm also quite a bit older than my sisters, so I never really had anybody to talk to as a child. I don't talk about my personal life to anybody really now, and I need to, I really think I need to sometimes. A cup of tea and a good chat is nice with a close friend.

We are awfully lucky, we have a very good standard of living. My life has turned out far better financially than I ever expected it to be. I never thought I would be able to afford Waterford crystal and to have so many lovely things: a beautiful home, designer clothes, nice furniture. It's hard work, the catering business, but it's really been worth it. I still hanker after the retail side of life, to come out from behind the scenes. But there it is, they say the grass is always greener on the other side.

Even though I'm surrounded by tea, I still enjoy a cup or two in the afternoons while I'm working. When the last customer has gone and the staff have finished clearing up, then I can relax, eat supper and have my evening treat—a cup of tea with a Danish pastry!

PERIWINKLE'S
VICTORIA SANDWICH
· · ·

"We are well known for our homemade cakes and you can't get more British than a Victoria sandwich. You can change the fillings for a little variety. If you visit Selworthy Green, come in for a cup of tea and say hello."

Chris Taylor

Victoria's Secret

1 cup / 250 g butter or
    margarine
1 cup / 200 g superfine sugar
    plus 1 tablespoon / 10 g for
    sprinkling

4 medium eggs, beaten
2 cups / 250 g self-rising flour,
    sifted
1 cup / 2.3 dl strawberry, raspberry
    or apricot jam or lemon
    curd for filling

Preheat your oven to 375°F/190° C. Lightly grease two 7-inch/18-cm round cake pans and line them with wax paper.

In a medium-sized bowl, cream the butter and the sugar together with a wooden spoon or a mixer until light in color and fluffy. Add the beaten eggs gradually, beating well. If curdling should happen, add a little of the flour. Gradually add the flour to the mixture, folding it in with a metal spoon and mixing it in thoroughly. Divide the mixture into the cake pans, smooth with a spatula for evenness and bake 20 to 25 minutes, until lightly golden brown. Cool for 10 minutes in the pans, then turn out and continue cooling on a wire rack. Lightly sprinkle the top of the best-shaped cake with the extra sugar.

When cool, spread the other cake with the filling of your choice and place the sugared cake on top.

Makes one 7-inch/18-cm cake; serves 8 to 10

SUGGESTED TEAS: Serve with a lighter tea: Darjeeling, Nilgiri or a green tea—Jasmine would be nice. Try a lemongrass herbal tea.

No, not a designer lingerie business—it's a delicious cake! The Victoria sandwich was actually named after Queen Victoria. Victoria adored tea parties, her dear husband Albert, and their nine children. Some other victorias: A victoria is also a low four-wheeled carriage with a folding top designed for two. And Victoria was the ancient Roman goddess of victory.

FRANCES FRY

PASSING THROUGH THE FRONT DOOR OF FRANCES FRY'S HOME is akin to walking into an art gallery: each wall of every room is covered with paintings. The majority are of horses, but there are donkeys, deer, cats and dogs as well. Additionally, a vast collection of ceramic, bronze and china statues top and fill every cupboard. Only the armchairs are naked of adornment. Frances is an artist who specializes in animals and landscapes. Most of the paintings decorating the house are her work. Her distinctive style is easily recognizable in the collection of oils and watercolours. It's detectable in many of the beautiful ceramics too. I find myself somewhat overwhelmed and amazed, yet totally appreciative of this display which shows a lifetime of dedication. As striking and as evident is the total passion that Frances has for horses. From the entrance hall, a rather grand, dark oak staircase directs you to the second floor of the house and to a sun-filled bedroom that has been converted into an art studio. Amongst the tubes of oils, brushes and piles of artwork is where Frances works and where we settled down for a private viewing of her art, a delightful chat and a cup of tea.

" Tea comes into its own for me if I've been out rambling with friends and we've had a good walk over the moors. Then we like to come back to one of those little places that do lovely cream teas."

A secret dell of springtime bluebells.

I'M SORRY TO ADMIT IT BUT I'M A coffee drinker rather than a tea drinker. We are a coffee household! We get through masses of coffee but not too many tea bags. I suppose you just grow up with one or the other, and that's that. Mother and I only have tea at teatime—half-past three to four o'clock—a cup of tea usually with a piece of Madeira cake. We buy our cakes in town at a very good bakery; I'm not much of a cook.

Tea comes into its own for me if I've been out rambling with friends and we've had a good walk over the moors. Then we like to come back to one of those little places that do cream teas. Tea is a pick-you-up when you're really tired. You work up a great appetite when you've been on a good walk. There are some lovely tea rooms around here. I think my favourite is at Horner. They give you masses of cream with your scones. At Horner it's a job to finish up every scrinch of jam and cream but we don't usually leave anything!

If I go on a long walk with friends we take a proper picnic, particularly in the summer. Last week I went out with a couple of friends and we had the most beautiful walk. We drove up to Brendon Cob, parked and walked all along Farley Water, then had our picnic down by the river. I was a bit aggrieved because I'd been telling these friends, "It's the most beautiful spot and you never see anybody there." Well, after our long hike we finally reached my secret picnicking spot only to find it absolutely swarming with at least a dozen overgrown Boy Scouts! I regarded this as a personal insult. We went trudging around the next bend in the river and it seemed to be peaceful there. No sooner had we laid out all our picnic things when six riders came along and decided to unsaddle their horses and have their picnic right next to us! It was still beautiful but in all the years I've gone there, I've never seen another soul, except on that day.

Our picnics are quite simple: ham and cucumber sandwiches, those little yogurt tubs you get from Marks & Spencer's, biscuits, bananas, and if it's a hot day, usually a cool soft drink. It's very nice to take a picnic if you get decent weather. As I said, I'm not a cook so it's all rather simple. I'm the one person who can't even boil an egg! I tend to be a bit absent-minded sometimes. I once put an egg on to boil without water in the saucepan! Oh, my! What a pong!

When I'm not out walking, taking photographs of animals or working on a painting commission on location, I'm in my art studio. I often paint all day. Lunch is at one and then I watch the news on the television after tea, which gives me somewhat of a break. In the summer I come back up here to the studio in the evening and do more work. In the winter you are restricted because of the limited daylight.

I've always been an artist. I started scribbling as soon as I could hold a pencil, and painting about the same time as I could read. I had a very nice art teacher, Miss Sturuck, she was very good. I went to The Lady Eleanor Holles School. It was a good academic school and had a very strict policy: all work. Compared to what I see school-children doing nowadays, I reckon we were deprived. We never had skiing trips and nice days out. However, I did enjoy my art class and when Miss Sturuck said draw your favourite subject, I would draw a horse. I have always loved horses. I like all animals, I think all animals are adorable when they are young. But horses, dogs and cats keep their grace and beauty all through their lives and so I rate those three as my favourites, in that order. I'm very lucky to be doing something that I like and to be able to make even a fairly precarious living at it. I dabble in a bit of writing, nature articles on cats and dogs, but mainly I stick to my art.

A naturally adorned rambler's hat.

Most of my painting commissions come from word-of-mouth. I'll paint someone's pony or horse and one of their friends admires it, and they will give me a ring and I'll go out to see their horse or whatever. I often go out to farms to do the rough sketches and take photographs. It helps to see the actual animal, particularly if the client wants an authentic view or something particular in the background. But you can't really do a terrific lot when you're there, you can just make detailed notes and colouring—for example, blaze cut halfway down, half a sock on the back left leg, things that you wouldn't always see on a photograph.

Evening light on an Exmoor Farm.

I've never been very happy with my portraits because I'm not a portrait painter. When I've had to include people I've had a couple of failures, but I reckon I can always get the animal satisfactorily.

I've always found animals far easier to understand than people. For instance, one day I got this telephone call from a woman wanting me to paint some of their family ponies for them. I met her a couple of days later in Exeter. She was very nice and we discussed the painting commission over a cup of tea. We settled on the following Wednesday for me to do my preliminary work. Most graciously she invited me to stop in for lunch at their home when my sketching was complete. Wednesday came and my mother and I went off to find their home. It was a huge old place the likes of which we had never seen before. The hall had a fabulous central staircase which was strewn with washing—pairs of jeans, shirts, underwear, every article of clothing you could imagine. You couldn't see the banister for all the clothes! The kitchen had to be seen to be believed, it was in absolute chaos. Dishes were piled everywhere, the sink was full of something, I'm not quite sure what. Every surface was loaded down with very odd things. I'm afraid I had to be terribly polite to swallow the lunch! We had an extremely indigestible piece of fish that was supposed to be haddock but definitely didn't look like it. The vegetables were a sort of pale mush on the plate. This main course was followed by a blackberry pie made with very underripe berries. It was just awful, some of the berries were still green! I was there to paint the children's ponies which was just lovely, but the house and the lunch, well, goodness gracious me!

I recall another time when Mother came along with me. We went into the most fabulous farmhouse. The sitting room, dining room and hall were immaculate, spotless and beautifully decorated. It was one of those charming, elegant farms. My work completed, I was having a break in the sitting room, relaxing in an extremely comfortable overstuffed armchair in front of the fire. I was just about to sip my tea when Mother came rushing into the room, hissing out of the corner of her mouth, "Don't drink the tea!" I had no idea what on earth was the matter. Well, I made some excuse about not being thirsty and I dragged Mother off to find out what was going on. Apparently she had taken a peep into their kitchen. It was an absolute pigsty. And if that wasn't enough to put one off one's tea, Mother grimaced as she told me what she had witnessed. The pet lamb, two dogs and four cats had all been drinking from the milk bottle that moments later was put on our tea tray!

I love my dogs and cats but they don't use our plates or the kitchen table to eat off and they don't have the run of the house either. They do sit with me every day in the studio. The Westy's

Two pints today, please.

Exmoor — a rambler's paradise.

getting old, bless him, and if he sees strangers now, he thinks he's going to the vet or something so he gets frightened. We make sure when visitors come he's tucked away. The Scotty on the other hand loves everybody, but he never knows when to stop loving, that's his trouble!

We've always had pets, dogs mainly. I wasn't a cat person until about ten years ago when a little stray black kitten decided to adopt me. I didn't have any say in the matter at all. His mother abandoned him on the greenhouse roof and he sat there meowing like a little seagull for three or four days. He watched us every time we came out of the back door with the scraps for the bird table. Of course I relented and let him have some bits and he immediately thought the welcome mat had officially been put out. He was my shadow from that moment on. Shadow absolutely converted me to cats. I had no idea they could be so loving and friendly. I lost Shadow about two or three years ago, but we have four of his family members around and about the place.

I spend quite a bit of time in the garden. It's a bit wild but it's a conservationist's garden, which covers a multitude of sins and lets you get away with a few acres of weeds. We do get beautiful butterflies because we have lovely nettles down by the compost heap. In spite of the fact that I know those nettles are there I always end up stinging myself, I never escape. I have to go in search of a dock leaf on most gardening days. Luckily we have docks in the garden too!

We live in a beautiful area. I walk out on the moors at every opportunity. I love the wildlife, the badger, the fox, the deer. If the weather's good you can spot deer most days. If you get really bad weather in the winter, it's not much good going out to the deer because they've got more sense than to be out on the open moor in foul weather! They're like us, they like a bit of shelter from the wind so they're more likely to be down hiding in the woods. If there's a nice afternoon they come out to get a bit of sun on their backs. If you know the right places you can stand a fair degree of luck in seeing them. Contrary to what most books tell you—that you can't spot deer at midday—if you know some of their favourite haunts, you can! They really like a good sunbathe, just like people. Over on Great Hill near Chetsford Water is a peat slide. I call it that because all the animals, the sheep especially, have worn away the vegetation and you've just got this fairly gentle slope covered in peat. Well, Peat Slide is one of the deer's favourite sunbathing spots. You get a nice warm day when you're on the lee side of the wind and you can sometimes find a herd of about thirty just lying out in the sun, enjoying it. If you creep up on them carefully they will be most obliging and settle back down to their sunbathing and leave you on the opposite hill, just sitting quietly looking at them, which is very nice.

One does have to be a bit careful out rambling. I was out with the ramblers walking from Porlock Weir up to Culbone last week and we had to cross a field that was full of cows and the most enormous bull. I know he's supposed to have his mind on other things when in with the cows, but my word, we did all cross that field rather sharpish. Bulls have this rather odd way of looking at you! You never quite know where you are with them. Our picnic was in a bit of a tumbled mess when we settled down to a sandwich and our tea on the safe side of the fence. We were so thankful for our thermos—a hot cup of tea is just the ticket to help calm the nerves after a bit of an incident.

Frances's wonderful boiled eggs are perfect for an egg sandwich recipe. Some other classic English sandwiches include cucumber, tomato, watercress, ham, smoked salmon with cream cheese and potted shrimp. You can get incredibly creative with the simple sandwich by adding all kinds of ingredients. Be daring—create your own special sandwiches, try adding chopped nuts, apples, raisins, herbs, spices, olives or mayonnaise to some of your favourite fillings.

Keep in mind: sandwiches do not store well. If you are not serving them immediately, keep the bread from becoming soggy by spreading the filling side with a very light layer of butter before adding the filling. Covering a plate of sandwiches with a clean damp tea towel (dish towel) is an ideal way to store them for up to an hour. The damp towel prevents the bread from drying out and the edges from curling.

FRANCES FRY'S
GUIDE TO BOILING AN EGG
. . .

"How to boil an egg might be considered a little basic by some, but it's rather fun to include. I trust you will all find it amusing. The egg and cress sandwich recipe sounds delicious, I think Michele must have discovered this in a tea shop somewhere. You can be sure it wasn't from me!"

Frances Fry

1. Make sure you fill the saucepan with enough water to cover the eggs you want to boil. (Eggs just don't boil well without this important ingredient.)

2. Put the saucepan on the stove and turn on heat.

3. When the water boils, carefully place fresh, newly laid free-range eggs, or if not available, regular large brown eggs, into the saucepan. (Free-range eggs have a delicious flavour and bright yellow colour.) Using a large spoon to ladle the eggs into the water helps to keep your fingers out of trouble.

4. Cook the eggs until done to your taste: 3 minutes for a soft egg, 15 minutes for hard-boiled.

5. Plunge eggs into cold water to cool—this helps to prevent black rings forming around the yolk.

EGG AND CRESS SANDWICHES

· · ·

2 hard-boiled eggs, cold
2 rounded tablespoons /
   30 ml mayonnaise
1 packet cress (if English cress
   is not available, alfalfa
   sprouts or alfalfa and
   clover mix)

Salt and pepper to taste
Butter or margarine, softened,
   for 6 slices of bread
6 thin slices bread, 3 white
   and 3 brown
Curry powder (optional)
Herbes de Provence (optional)

Shell your eggs and grate on your cheese grater (medium holes). Add the mayonnaise and mix well. Add some of the cress (snip off with scissors) and mix in. Season with salt and pepper to taste. Spread the mixture onto lightly buttered white bread, add a thin layer of cress and top with a slice of lightly buttered brown bread. Trim off the crusts and cut each sandwich into 4 small triangles. For an assortment try adding curry powder to one batch of egg salad and herbes de Provence to another. Season to your taste.

Makes 12 small triangle sandwiches

SUGGESTED TEAS: Serve with Orange Pekoe tea, iced in the summer. It's a sweet tea and delicious hot or cold. If you like a more pungent tea, try Ceylon; it's a bright golden-coloured tea, good with lemon and lovely iced. Make ice cubes out of cold tea and add them to your iced tea to keep it cold and undiluted. To add a touch of pizazz, freeze a small edible flower blossom or mint leaf in each cube.

WINIFRED WESTCOTT

*A*FTER PASSING THE VILLAGE CHURCH IN BROMPTON REGIS, BUT well before you get to Exton Hill, is a stretch of roadway called Sanctuary Lane. It's narrow and very steep and must be taken at a snail's pace. Before you reach the crest of the hill, a small sign is nestled in the hawthorn hedge. The wooden sign, which is easily missed, could use another coat of varnish but the bold letters clearly state Higher Foxhanger Farm, and this is where, a half-dozen years ago, I first met Mrs. Winnie Westcott. It was Christmastime and a cold chill filled the December air, but Winnie's kitchen was overflowing with warmth and friendliness when I was invited in for a cup of tea. It was baking day, a plate piled high with golden scones was on the table and Winnie's reputation for delicious clotted cream was confirmed by the bowlful of thick yellow cream that sat next to the scones. Besides the welcome heat of the coal-burning oven and the aroma of baking, scores of Christmas cards filled the room, hung on strings laced back and forth across the kitchen ceiling. Decorated with scenes of the hunt, carollers, sheep in snowdrifts and holly-topped plum puddings, they had come from all over Great Britain, from Land's End to John o'Groat's. Several years have passed since that first welcome in December. We have shared many pots of tea together over the years, and perhaps, too many cream-filled scones. The kitchen armchair in the corner where Winnie's husband

"We always have our afternoon tea, mind you. If you don't keep the inner man going, you can't keep the outer one going, can you?"

sat is now empty. Bill and Winnie used to have a busy home full of bed-and-breakfast guests who returned year after year to the Westcotts' warm hospitality. Bill's worn seat is now occupied by a black cat. It too enjoys an afternoon nap, the warmth of the fire and the comfort of the ticking wall clock. William is missed.

Today Winnie made ready the already spotless dairy for inspection, her modern equipment gleaming alongside the old-fashioned wooden tools proudly displayed. Accompanying the scones, jam and cream were a crusty loaf of bread, curls of farmhouse yellow butter and a rich fruitcake.

I WAS BORN IN 1913. THE MILK SCALD THAT DAY, Father said. This year, I will be in Scotland for my birthday and I shall have a drink that day. Not a whiskey mind you, no that's too strong. I'm not against nobody having a drink, in a seasonable polite way. I don't like to see anybody drink and get drunk. If I see a drunk man, I've got to watch him closely from then on. I've never seen a drunk woman, no not a woman that's gone that far, and I've been farming all my life and lived right here most of it.

This farm was built in 1916. I moved in as a new bride in 1944. We had no roads, no conveniences in them days. There were woods on all sides of the farm then.

I first made cream and butter when I was a young girl, goodness me yes, made it all me life. We never sat down unless we had cream and butter on the table. My mother, before she died, she'd have told you this. She never bought a pound of butter, she never bought a pound of cream, she never bought a pound of lard, she never bought a pound of jam, she never bought milk or eggs and she never bought a man's shirt, she learnt dressmaking, so she made them. It was very hard work in the old days.

I have won many a prize for my cream and butter, but I'm not keen on showing too much. I like the judgment of me customers.

If they say, "Winnie, we keep your cream over a week, nearly a fortnight," that's enough praise for me. I always have won prizes, but I've stopped entering now, you have to let the younger ones come on, not grab all yourself.

I can't give you no time at all about how long it takes to make clotted cream. I does it with my own judgment. You can't have the heat too low for cream because you mustn't delay it too long, cream wants to be done up fairly quickly and slowed down to finish. But not slow at the start. As long as it's not boiling, that's the main thing, you must watch the cream don't boil. I've done it so much, you don't do

Winnie's prize-winning butter and clotted cream.

time, you just do it by sight. You scald it then you let it cool. When the head's up yellow, then it's finished. I make cream every day. If you want a taste yourself or anybody, when you go to the fridge the cream's ready for which way you want it.

If you've got a bit extra on hand, just put a spoonful of clotted cream in your cake mix, makes the cake lighter, doesn't it! It doesn't matter what, you can mix cream in everything. If I've got any boiled potatoes over, I take they potatoes, I mash 'em with a spoonful of butter or cream and then with an ice-cream scoop, scoop 'em out, put they on a dish and you bake they, they're lovely. When I used to have visitors staying here, it didn't mind what pudding [dessert] it was, I always had a dish of cream on the table. Fruit, pastry pies, cake, steamed pudding, it doesn't matter, we always put the cream on. Mind you, never put clotted cream on your face to keep it soft, it'll make your face hairy! And never put cream on toast, the heat destroys the cream an' 'tis soon gone. Do you know, years ago I used to come home from school, sit down to meals with sometimes no meat on the plate. Mother had the vegetables with a great plop of butter or cream on they. Just vegetables, I like that. I grow all me own veg.

I've no time for what doctors has to say about that cholesterol, I love butter, eggs and cream. Butter you have to stir by hand. It's a wonderful bit of work, butter. You take cream as it is and put it in the tub. The tub's an invention from the old people. I've seen roses and everything carved in butter, made out of all butter they are, it can easily be done with practise. Years ago my children gave me what they thought was a real butter pat. I said, "Thank you very much but it's not right." They said, "What's wrong, Mum?" I told em, 'At the handle down to the base of the butter pat, there should be a hole, so you can blow down it.' That relieves butter from the pat. They make them today without that hole, and that's no butter pat. Today they call these tools antiques and I use them now, and I'm still living. They're no antiques to me. I make enough for home and to sell on to regular customers. I sell me butter, cream, eggs and yogurt too now.

We always have our afternoon tea, mind you. If you don't keep the inner man going you can't keep the outer one going, can you? At half-past five, twenty to six, I like to sit down and have me tea and listen to the news, do two jobs in one that way, see. I have a couple of poached eggs on toast with a cup of tea. Tea today is like dust, you don't see real tea leaves in it. Years ago old people would read the tea in the cups but there's no leaves now. Sometimes I have tea and a piece of cake. Yes, I make me own cake. The other day Dennis [my dairyman] said, "Winnie, what's your weights?" "I don't know, I do

No clotted cream? Thick whipping cream makes a rich and delicious substitute.

it by guess," I told him. He said, "Do you put proper cream in your cakes?" I said "If I've got plenty, it goes in!" I use me own butter, milk an' eggs. You don't put much milk in once you've got the eggs in. I tell you what I do like in a cake, you get 'em at the county stores, raisins. Some people don't like them mind. If you cut them the flavour goes in the cake. You just run your knife through the raisins and that cake'll come out lovely. I'm old-fashioned, I don't buy much from the stores. I used to make my own bread but I buy that now. I always made a nine-pound loaf. You have to have it big if you've got a large family. It's not like today's bread. It was weighty, more substantial, so you didn't eat slice after slice.

There was always gossip at the meal table. Everything would come home, mealtimes. We'd talk about anything; going to market, neighbouring farms, our animals, lambing, shearing, ploughing, all manner of work. Funerals were always talked about. If you had a wonderful garden you were remembered and buried with respect. There was more talk at table than anywhere. You must remember we children, when we were small, we weren't allowed to talk at table. No, we just had to listen to what was going on. What the weather was going to do and everything. If the cat had its back to the fire, then it would be a cold day followin'. We learnt about country ways there. Your kitchen table was a meetingplace for business and learn-ing. Oh yes, it don't matter what it was, it was all talked about at the table with family.

At Christmastime, one great-aunt used to send us half a crown. We divided this half crown between the three of us children, and what do you think we used to call our great-aunt? Well, we got tenpence each, there were four farthings to the penny, so she was called Aunty Forty Farthings. But we dare not say it to her face. I wanted to spend my money on presents for Mother, Father, my brother and sister and Uncle Bert. I remember I bought Mother a thimble. In those days you used to get a sugary sweet in the shape of a clock with a face painted on it, and I got them too. They were beautiful, real sugar. I didn't have

There was always gossip at the meal table.

nothing for myself but I had a present each for they. I felt proud to give them something each for Christmas. You never saw an orange in the shops on regular days, they were only for Christmastime. When you went down to Scott's the grocer, you saw all the dried fruits weighed up by them and put in bags ready for the puddings and pies. Oh, Mother made a fine Christmas pudding, delicious to the taste. I know it was a hard life years ago, but you had better food.

Mother was a Ridd, oh yes. You'll have a hard time finding folk from the West Country that's not heard of the Ridds. Mother came from Martinhoe by Woody Bay near Lynton. Martinhoe's a dead place now, it was a lively place one time. Yes, mother was a Ridd, she was one of ten living. Half boys and half girls and there's no great-grandsons at all. One time Mother was here when I had visitors staying and they asked her if she had read R. D. Blackmore's book *Lorna Doone*. "Miss Ridd what do you think of the famous book?" they asked. She said, "Have you read the book?" "Yes," they said. "Then you know as much as I!" She didn't talk about it much. It's a lovely book, Grandfather's described in it. Oh yes, he's

there, a very thickset man. His sons all went in the First World War. That family has farmed the Martinhoe farm for three generations. All the Ridds are connected if you go back, I think you'll find they all come from one branch. A big family the Ridds, they believed in big families back in those days.

Winnie's farm kitchen was overflowing with warmth and friendliness when I was invited in for a cup of tea.

69

Higher Foxhanger farm practises only healthy, old-fashioned farming techniques.

I do real farming at Higher Foxhanger, I know what's going in my ground. I don't believe in putting all these chemicals in the fields and in your livestock feed. Oh my dear 'tis awful. Putting a few wild seeds in, that's not organic, it's not! Food today, I don't know! If you buy a biscuit, it's like buying the barley meal, you don't taste no real biscuit. You know years ago, when Mary was a baby—she was my firstborn—I used to feed her with a biscuit soaked in milk and she came along lovely with that. I'd spoon the biscuit mix in her, with an apostle teaspoon, they're a very small spoon. At the end of the handle, there's an apostle. I had half a dozen given me on our wedding day. They're used for teas, just for teas, but I did use one for feeding the babies.

My hobbies are me animals really, but I've always enjoyed the Young Farmers. They've got me on the advisory board. Sometimes things come up and you can help them, the young ones. Every year they come and sing Christmas carols to me. Last Christmas there were so many here that one bottle of sherry didn't go round. I also give good support to the Village Hall. I think the Hall is the mainstay of the village, it keeps the people together, makes a community, which keeps your country together. You go to some villages without a Village Hall and they're empty places. Years ago we didn't go out of Brompton for anything, only for the doctor. We had the policeman, the undertaker, the butcher, the baker, the vicar, two cooks; we had the lot here. It was a different life altogether, it used to be so alive in the small villages. We used to ride horses so we didn't go too far, you see.

I like to put my time to producing good food. It's a busy day but there's nothing wrong with it, I'm no idle woman. I don't think you'd find someone to call me that, no. Washing and cleaning the house on Monday, Tuesday I wash the cream jars and utensils, Wednesday I do the eggs, clean them up, Thursdays I get ready for Fridays and Fridays we deliver to all the regular customers. There's jobs done every day; makin' cream, feeding and cleaning out the poultry and cooking. When the weather's good and time allows I'm out in the garden. I try to get a bit of a rest on a Sunday but that doesn't always happen. It's a hard life, but you get your enjoyment afterward.

I've got many to admire, for one my mother. She was hard on us but that was the right way to do it, you see this as you get older. My dears, I'll tell you one of the things Mother taught me. It's good sound sense, listen to these words. Never marry a man who puts his hands in his pockets, cause he'll be a lazy man. Oh yes! Never marry a man who does that. God rest his soul, my William never put his hands in his pockets.

Thick whipping cream, a tasty substitute for clotted cream (notice the apostle spoon).

71

WINNIE'S COUNTRY SCONES

. . .

"Scones are lovely with cream and homemade strawberry jam. We usually get a lovely crop of strawberries from the garden, and I put up quite a bit of me own jam. We never have store-bought, oh no! Raspberry is good but strawberry is best with scones. I like a cup of tea and a freshly baked scone in the afternoon."

Winnie Westcott

What Is Clotted Cream?

It's a thick, rich yellow cream, famous to the West Country of England. It is lavishly dolloped on scones, cakes, fresh fruit salad, pies, practically every sweet or pudding enjoyed in this region. Made in huge quantities commercially, this delicious cream is shipped all over England. Equally scrumptious is farmhouse clotted cream, a handmade cream that tends to be a richer yellow and slightly thicker in consistency than the commercial variety. In many farmhouse kitchens the clotted cream pan sits solidly on the warm Aga (a coal-burning stove) waiting patiently for its milky contents to separate. The cream rises

2 cups / 250 g all-purpose flour
¼ teaspoon / 1 g salt
½ cup / 125 g butter or margarine
2 level teaspoons / 8 g cream of tartar
1 level teaspoon / 4 g baking soda

1 teaspoon / 4 g baking powder
½ cup / 100 g superfine white sugar
2 eggs, medium size
4 to 6 tablespoons / 60 to 90 ml milk

Preheat your oven to 425° F / 220° C. Lightly grease a baking sheet. Sift the flour and salt into a large bowl. With your fingers, lightly rub in the butter or margarine. Sift the cream of tartar and baking soda if lumpy, then add with the rest of the dry ingredients to the bowl. Lightly beat the eggs and add to the mixture. Add enough milk to make a light dough. On a lightly floured surface roll out the dough to about 1 inch / 2.5 cm thick. Cut into rounds with a 2-inch / 5-cm cookie cutter. Place on baking sheet and bake 10 to 15 minutes, until well risen and golden.

Serve warm, straight from the oven. Scones do not keep well. Eat them on baking day, cut in half horizontally. Spread the bottom half with a layer of jam then a good spoonful of cream, and top with the other half of the scone.

Makes 10 to 12 scones

SUGGESTED TEAS: A strong cup of tea—Indian is what we drink on the farm. I like loose tea—it's hard to find tea with good leaves these days.

WINNIE'S STRAWBERRY JAM

. . .

3½ pounds / 1,75 k firm
    and ripe strawberries,
    hulled

Juice of 1 large lemon
2 pounds / 1,5 k sugar

In a large saucepan, gently heat the strawberries and the lemon juice. Stir constantly to reduce the volume. Add the sugar, stirring until completely dissolved. Boil until the jam reaches the setting point, 222° F/105° C. Remove any scum from the surface with a metal spoon. Leave the jam undisturbed to cool until a skin forms on the surface and the fruit sinks to the bottom, about 25 minutes. Stir gently to mix the strawberries. Ladle into warm, dry jars and seal with melted paraffin.

Serve when set and cold on Winnie's Country Scones, bread and butter or toast, or use as a filling for a Victoria sandwich or for jam tarts.

Makes 5 pounds/2,5 k of jam

to the top of the milk and is skimmed off the top. Wandering the country lanes of Somerset and Devon you will spot numerous farm gates with handmade signs, CLOTTED CREAM FOR SALE. It's great fun to brave the farmyard dog, be invited into the kitchen and buy a jar or two.

Unless you can get milk straight from the cow, don't bother trying to make clotted cream from American milks and creams, it's hopeless. What you can do, however, is whip up heavy whipping cream until it's really thick and spreadable (don't add sugar or vanilla). It is not the same as clotted cream but is very delicious all the same.

HAYLEY RICHARDS

NICHOLLS FARM IS UNUSUAL BECAUSE OF ITS LOCATION. It's bang smack in the center of a small English village. You can hear the church bells ringing on Sunday mornings—the church is right next door. The combination village post office and shop is just across the road, and the local teenagers hang out around the wood gate at the entrance of the farm—because the village phone box is located there. But go out of the back door of the farm and it's another world: fields and woods as far as the eye can see, cows, chickens, sheep and the trusty family pony. Nicholls Farm has masses of room for childhood adventures and is not at all isolated from the goings-on of the village as many farms are. Hayley Richards has lived here all her life. The perfect day for six-year-old Hayley is inviting two favourite chums over for an afternoon of digging through the dressing-up trunk, using every shade of lipstick and eye shadow from Mummy's old makeup bag, followed by a floury baking session at the kitchen table, where culinary masterpieces are created in vast quantities, and finally collapsing on the tartan blanket for tea on the lawn. This is Hayley's heaven.

"I have one sugar in my tea and milk. My best tea mug is the one with the teddy on it." Hayley (on right with pigtails) with her very best chums, Emily and Alexandra.

Teatime with Hayley's toys.

Hayley (with white hood) as Mary, Nativity school play.

MUMMY MAKES TEA FOR US, I LIKE NICE CHOCOLATE biscuits, ham sandwiches, sausage rolls, chocolate cake—Mummy doesn't make that, we get it from the lady at the post office. She makes yummy cakes and Mummy says it's not worth *her* time making them. The lady at the post office has a really loud voice but I like her because she lets me go there and play and she makes lovely cakes. I have one sugar in my tea and milk. My best tea mug is the one with the teddy on it. Sometimes I use James's mug but he usually doesn't let me. Pinkie Poodle drinks tea, he's my very own teddy bear. He's pink and has a black nose. My pound puppies like cake better than tea, but when they are naughty they have to miss teatime and go to their room.

My brothers can have one biscuit each, but that's all! My dog, Bruno, gets the heads of the gingerbread princes. I don't like eating that part, so he gets them. I like to make princes because you can dress them up with currants and icing sugar. My favourite is to make princesses but we only have a gingerbread-man cutter and it's hard to make skirts for girl gingerbreads.

Sometimes I go to birthday teas and we have jelly [jello]. Red jelly is my favourite flavour. Mrs. Sinclaire's tummy wobbles just like jelly when she runs after her dog. Her dog always fights with Bruno, so I hate him. Bruno's the best sheep dog in the world.

James and Gregory are my brothers, James is eight, he's older than me. Gregie is only four, I'm older than him and my sister is called Rachele, she is a baby. I love them and my mummy and daddy.

James can make tea, I can't, I'm not allowed yet. He makes tea for Mummy and Daddy on their birthdays. He spills it on the carpet when he goes upstairs. Mummy likes tea in bed. I never have it, we have to sit at the table and drink ours. When I grow up I'm going to eat a lot more chocolate and have tea in bed too.

76

HAYLEY'S GINGERBREAD PRINCES
. . .

"I make these for my mummy and my daddy. Sometimes my friends come to play after school and we dress up and have a tea party together. My favourite is when my cousin Emily comes, she's ten, I'm six. Emily has a little dog named Poppy, she licks everyone. I don't like to eat the heads of my gingerbread princes so I give them to our dog Bruno, he loves them!"

Hayley Richards

Hayley loves to cut out and decorate the gingerbread princes. This is what she calls "making them." Adult participation and supervision are needed.

To transform her gingerbread men into princes, Hayley uses currants, icing sugar, cherries, chocolate drops and anything else she can find in the larder. You can use an icing bag to pipe on the faces, clothes and crowns.

> 3 tablespoons / 45 ml honey
> ¾ cup / 150 g dark brown sugar
> Grated rind of 1 medium-sized
>   lemon (yellow zest only, not
>   white pith) and a few drops
>   of lemon juice
> ½ cup / 125 g butter
> 2 cups / 250 g all-purpose
>   flour plus more for flouring
>   the board
> 2 teaspoons / 8 g ground ginger
> Pinch of ground cinnamon

Preheat your oven to 325° F/160° C. Grease a baking sheet.

In a saucepan over a low heat, slowly warm the honey, brown sugar and lemon rind and juice until the sugar has dissolved. Add the butter and stir until it melts. Then remove from heat and stir in the flour, ginger and cinnamon. Mix well to a stiff dough.

Roll out to about ¼-inch/.5-cm thickness on a lightly floured board. Using a special gingerbread-man cutter, cut out the princes. Place on baking sheet and bake 15 to 20 minutes. Cool, then decorate.

Makes 10 to 12 medium-sized princes

SUGGESTED TEAS: For children, any herbal tea they like. Try an iced lemon herb tea for summer picnics. Fill the glass with iced tea, stir in sugar or honey and add a squeeze of lemon. As an extra treat use a lemon lollypop or lemon sweet stick to stir it all up—Mummy.

VIRGINIA, LADY BATH

MARCHIONESS OF BATH

IN 1953 VIRGINIA PENELOPE PARSONS MARRIED ONE OF THE MOST famous faces in English aristocracy, Henry Thynne, the sixth marquess of Bath. During the past four decades Virginia has been hostess to British royalty, dignitaries from around the world and the millions of visitors who have toured the family estate. Her lovely face has been seen on television and in newspapers and magazines, and is familiar to many

"I like good old English tea. I say English, but it isn't really, it's Indian. We've had the same black tea invariably for years. I won't have anything else. I don't like the flavour of China tea."

British people. Alexander, Virginia's stepson, is now the seventh marquess of Bath, and he resides at Longleat, the stately home of the Thynne family. Longleat has been a huge part of Lady Bath's life. One must know her beloved Longleat to know and understand the sixth marchioness of Bath. In the spring of 1540, John Thynne paid £53 (approximately $80 today) for 60 acres of Wiltshire land known as the priory of Longleat. When Henry Thynne, Lord Bath, inherited the estate in the twentieth century, it was in financial ruin, yet he was determined to keep and maintain his family's home. In 1949 Longleat became the first privately owned stately home in England to open its doors to the public on a regular basis. Tours of the 118-room home have delighted visitors from all over the world. Equally popular are the famous "lions of Longleat" which roam freely in the safari park nestled in the heart of the 16,000-acre estate. The late Lord Bath's imaginative solutions to the huge financial

Longleat on a misty morning.

challenges he faced over fifty years ago have proven a total success. Henry and Virginia's dream has been kept alive. Longleat remains in the Thynne family, is a national tourist attraction and is acknowledged as one of the most beautiful stately homes in England.

Unlike Henry, Virginia never lived at Longleat. When she and Lord Bath married they moved into Jobs Mill, a sixteenth-century mill house a few miles from Longleat. The Mill was in a shambles but Virginia quickly went to work and created a home that is now as elegant as it is comfortable. However magnificent Longleat is, the more intimate, romantic Mill is the perfect setting for this lady: the soft roll of the lawns, the dovecote, the shaded flower beds, the boathouse and the sleepy river with its resident pair of English swans. Jobs Mill was originally a corn or silk mill during its working life; now the river curls through the acres of lawn and flows under the library of a lovely English home.

In front of a crackling fire in the sitting room, I listen for the ripple of water. "No," Lady Bath tells me, "you can only hear the river in the library, it's just a foot or two under the floorboards." Meanwhile the tea table is set, beautiful china holding scrumptious teatime delights appears and tea is poured. In the glow of the fire, Virginia (as the marchioness encourages me to call her) and I settle comfortably into overstuffed armchairs, relaxing into our afternoon and the enjoyment of a formal English tea.

WHEN WE MOVED INTO JOBS MILL OVER FORTY YEARS ago, it was in a frightful mess. We had to take out the staircase, the window frames, it really was quite frightful. I did so enjoy the deco-

Jobs Mill.

rating aspect—selecting the fabrics, paint shades and wallpapers. I wouldn't like to have somebody else do it for me no matter how wrong it was. I'd rather not have someone design for me. There go the doves! [Looking through the small square windowpanes into the garden, we watch a flutter of white feathers.] Their dovecote was blown over in that awful storm we had a few months ago and they now spend quite a bit of time on the roof of the boot room. When the back door from the boot room is opened, twenty or so beautiful doves are airborne in an

A few of Longleat's treasures.

instant. It's really quite lovely. Perhaps the cook is needing some herbs from the kitchen garden and has gone for a stroll?

When the grandchildren come for tea it is usually mugs and trays, not at all formal. Far more relaxing for everyone that way really. Besides enjoying the tea and cakes they love all the animals we have here—the ducks, chickens, dogs and goats. Our swans have just had cygnets. The proud parents come up to the house for their corn breakfast every morning. Feeding the swans really starts the day off.

I get up around eightish. My breakfast is a bowl of Alpen, it's a wonderful cereal. I have a man who cooks for me, a dear man, but I don't eat a large English breakfast, mine is quite simple. I go to Longleat probably every other day. I do all the buying for Lady Bath's Gift Shop. We have what's called a coordinator, and she does all the shop management, thank goodness, while I go all over the place to buy things. I have *Lady Bath's Cookbook* and that seems to do very well in the shop, and the prints of my watercolour paintings sell steadily too. You have your successes and your failures in buying for a shop. It can be a bit of a worry.

The originals of my watercolours are all at Longleat in the old library at the top of the house. On rainy days like today you can't putter about in the garden, so I do my painting. I've got a little desk by the window in the other room where I paint in the afternoons. The cat invariably comes and parks with me, as cats do. She's quite content to sit on my lap while I work. I am so thankful I went to art school, it helps now in drawing and painting my flowers. Drawing used to be my favourite art form, but I think it's watercolour now. I can't get off painting flowers, they are my favourite. Once you specialize you can't get away from it. Art means an awful lot to me. I suppose it's the most important thing after my family, home and garden. I love it so much.

I love the spring flowers. Tulips and daffodils are my favourites although I must include roses as well, because they are so adorable, aren't they? And they smell so lovely. I have a few but I'm ashamed of them, roses just don't do at all well here. That's a "Caroline Testus" in the vase, she grows on the kitchen wall. She's the only one that does quite well at all. The dear gardener is successful with every-thing else. The herbaceous border is quite lovely, and is at its peak in June when we have the garden open to the public.

Lady Bath's garden.

"I love spring flowers, tulips are a favourite."

Afternoon tea is quite a tradition in the family. We've always had tea, always. With my grandmother and mother, all through my life. That's just our tradition. Having a nice cosy cup of tea with the family. Even if I'm on my own, I always have tea and a little something to eat with it at five o'clock. It's a gathering time for the family, very much exclusive to teatime. When it's fine, we have tea outside, we take the trolley out laden up with all the tea things.

Marilyn, the wife of the cook, makes the most delicious poppyseed cake. My daughter Silvy and I adore it, it is rather different. On Fridays after I have my hair done, I always go to the WI [Women's Institute] stall at the Village Hall. They have wonderful cakes there. They're so good it really rather stops one from trying to make cakes at home. They look so wholesome and lovely, quite different from shop cakes. In the winter we have crumpets toasted in front of the fire. Christmas is a special time too. We always have Christmas cake at teatime on Christmas Day.

I like good old English tea. I say English, but it isn't really, it's Indian. We've had the same black tea invariably for years and years. I won't have anything else. I don't like China tea. When people give it to me at a tea party I drink it but I don't care for it at all really. We usually have a sandwich at teatime, all sorts, tomato sandwiches, cucumber, any old thing that comes to mind. And toast, a lot of toast especially in the winter, with damson jam or perhaps Gentlemen's Relish (an anchovy paste).

There is Goosey. He's such a beauty. That goose arrived one day while Henry and I were sitting at breakfast. Suddenly, this enormous thing came in through the garden door. To this day I have no idea where he came from. He's been here for about nine years. Sadly, Goosey has never been too lucky with his wives. Something always happens to them. I think this one is his third! It's rather a good thing because a lot of goslings about the place wouldn't be too good for the garden.

Our children know, whatever happens, at five I am invariably home for tea. They all think of tea rather like I do really. It's a tradition they would hate to be broken. I know my daughter Silvy always has tea at her home. Silvy told me she felt just awful the other day when her family had to dash up to London and couldn't stop in. It was five o'clock and they hated driving by, knowing we would be in here having tea!

Things that take time seem to be disappearing—writing letters, hand-sewing and taking afternoon tea. We have been so fortunate to keep our afternoon tradition. Henry so enjoyed a cup of tea at five o'clock.

Lord Bath, my darling Henry, what lovely and precious memories. I suppose I didn't fall in love with Henry straightaway, no, it was on the second or third meeting. There was something about him. I overheard somebody saying he was so glamorous. I thought, "Hum, glamorous!" I think that was the first clue. I would never have left my first husband if it hadn't been for Henry. It was during the war, so many people were separated then.

Henry and I fell in love, we were in love for quite some time, several years before we married. It was all very, very difficult. And then finally, you know, one thought, "Well, we must be together."

The boathouse at Jobs Mill.

A corner of Longleat's kitchen.

Divorce is awful, you go through so much, don't you. I've been very fortunate with my husbands. Now, I have my children and grandchildren, and of course my adorable Maria, my Cavalier King Charles spaniel. I think I am very, very fortunate.

I suppose I am a romantic, and I'm quite strong-willed. When I set myself to do something, I try and do it. I am pretty happy, really. I don't have terrible depressions or anything. I am easy to get along with, but I would say on the other hand I'm a loner. I would much prefer to be at home than at a party for instance. I'm not a gregarious person at all. I loved parties when I was young but I've always been shy.

The biggest accomplishment in my life was getting over my shyness, that and helping with Longleat, helping Henry. Overcoming my shyness was just a sort of gradual thing, always pushing myself, I suppose. But I didn't really get out of shyness until well into my first marriage. Then, when I married Henry, I felt very shy all over again, because I had to compete with Longleat and all the publicity. And then I gradually got over that and now I feel as happy as anything doing all these things.

Becoming the sixth marchioness of Bath was a bit intimidating at first. I think it's rather nice to be a ladyship. But otherwise there's really nothing very special to it. I've always refused to make speeches. I suppose I could do it, but it would make me feel so awful for two or three days beforehand, so I've always refused. My shyness is still there with any public speaking. Henry and I did a lot of public relations work at Longleat, meeting various people, doing television interviews, that sort of thing. In 1980, 407 years after Queen Elizabeth I stayed at Longleat, Queen Elizabeth II and her family came for a visit to participate in the celebration of Longlete's quarter-centenary. But life is much quieter today. More tea, my dear?

Afternoon tea continues to be at five o'clock at Jobs Mill, on sunfilled days or on rainy ones. There's often a blazing fire in the hearth, welcoming and warming. There's even that favourite bottle of Henry's special whiskey on the sideboard. Lady Bath is a gracious hostess, but there's something missing; it's just not quite the same without him. Henry Thynne, the sixth marquess of Bath—"Little H" is dearly missed.

THE MARCHIONESS OF BATH'S
BLUE POPPYSEED CAKE
· · ·

"At five o'clock I take a break from my painting and enjoy a cup of tea and a slice of cake in the sitting room. We invariably have afternoon tea at five. Blue Poppyseed Cake is one of the family favourites. I hope you and your family all enjoy it as much as we do."

Virginia, Lady Bath

¾ cup/140 g blue poppyseeds
1 cup/250 ml whole milk
1 cup/250 g butter or
    margarine
1 cup/200 g light brown
    sugar

3 large eggs, separated
2 cups/250 g plain wheat
    flour
1 ¼ teaspoons/5 g baking
    powder

Preheat your oven to 350° F/175° C. Grease and line an 8-inch/20-cm round cake pan with greaseproof paper.

In a saucepan over low heat, bring the poppyseeds to a boil in the milk. Turn off the heat and let them soak for 25 minutes, covered.

In a mixing bowl, cream the butter or margarine and sugar together until light and fluffy, by hand with a wooden spoon or with a mixer. Add the egg yolks one at a time and beat in thoroughly. Mix the flour and baking powder together and fold into creamed mixture. Stir in the soaked poppyseeds and milk. Whisk the egg whites until stiff and fold them carefully into the batter. Spoon into the pan and bake until the center of the cake feels firm and a skewer comes out clean, 1½ hours. Let the cake stand for 10 minutes in the pan, then turn out on a cooling rack.

Makes one 8-inch/20-cm cake; serves 8 to 12

SUGGESTED TEAS: Serve with Darjeeling tea. Darjeeling, with its delicate flowery flavour is grown in the mountain areas around the town of Darjeeling in northeastern India. It has a distinctive bouquet which is somewhat fruity. Considered one of the finest teas, it complements this delicious cake beautifully. Darjeeling can be served with milk and sugar or black with or without lemon.

ELIZABETH BROOKS

D. J. MILES & CO., TEA AND COFFEE MERCHANTS IS A FAMILY-OWNED business located in the small country village of Porlock. You won't see magazine ads or television commercials for this local favourite. Miles Tea Merchants have a very simple system of marketing: visitors come to the area, drink Miles tea, and before you can shake a tea bag, these same visitors are walking down the lane to the tea merchant's to buy their own supply. Elizabeth Brooks assists the owners with the mountain of paperwork that accumulates in the office above the workroom. But at tea-break time Liz is putting the kettle on and joining the tea-packing ladies downstairs at the large table in the center of the room for laughter, stories, gossip and packet after packet of biscuits. Liz is thirty-three, divorced, has three children and lives on a farm with Robert, who has four children. Every other weekend all the clan converge on the farm. Kate at eleven is the oldest child, two of the boys are nine and there's one each at five, six, seven and eight. Life has dramatically changed during the past few years for these two families, but there's nothing new in regard to the friendships. The children have known one another since they were very small. One thing is guaranteed: two adults and seven children make it extremely lively around the Sunday afternoon tea table.

"Sunday afternoon is special to us. This is the time when we sit down to a proper tea. The children go back to their other families after tea, so it's a lovely way for us all to be together at teatime."

A springtime welcome home.

ROBERT IS A LOCAL MAN, A SCHOOLTEACHER. His father farms and we live in his massive thatched farm-house. The house is on the roadside, with a stone porch that's always full of Wellies. There's a few other bits and bobs floating around as well, but the kids always line up their boots in pairs by the front door. It's a landmark and most people find us by the Wellies!

Sunday afternoon is special for us. This is the time when we sit down to a proper tea. The children go back home to their other families after tea, so it's a lovely way for us all to be together before they leave. You can always count on Sunday teatime at our house, with a vast pot of tea. It's the one time we actually have the entire family sitting down together. The children want to be together, and the time they spend here with us is the only time they can see one another.

My children live with their father, which is not an ideal situation for me but I don't really have much choice. I've always had a full-time job and it just worked out that he kept the children. They're in their own home and their own school. We've tried to keep the changes to a minimum for them, which was the main thing. I see them during the week and on weekends. You make more of an effort when you don't have them with you all the time. I find I don't put things off like I used to. In the past I'd say, "I'll do it in a minute." Not any more. Now it's "Right, do it now."

My life is very full, never a dull moment, especially on week-ends. It's a bit hectic then, what with ballet, horse riding cross-country races and cricket matches. With the children getting ready to go back home on Sunday afternoons, taking showers and packing, it's amazing we have time for tea! The kids' favourite tea consists of hot crusty rolls, chocolate fudge cake, crisps, mini–chocolate chip bis-cuits and bread and butter with homemade jam; they're quite into that. And jelly and ice cream too! That's the standard tea, I don't think I dare vary it. They all sit there ravenous, waiting for it to arrive on the table. I sometimes make a speckled tea loaf which is a delicious cakey bread. But I'm not really very domesticated, I don't often bake cakes. And of course, we only drink Miles tea in our house.

I've learnt a lot about tea since I first started working for Miles four years ago. I'm the general dogsbody or jack-of-all-trades. I work in the office and I can pack tea and coffee, I've done all that. I used to think making tea was a simple process—the tea leaves were picked, dried and chopped up, that was it. Now I know how involved it is, from where it's grown at the fabulous tea gardens to tea purchasing, tea tasting and tea blending.

Miles's don't need to advertise as such. It's very much word-of-mouth business. We sell all over England but funnily enough, not in London. Most of the hotels, bed-and-breakfasts and cafes around here serve Miles tea. It's a good strong cup of tea, it's not weak. People come to stay here in the area, taste our tea and we end up posting it to new customers all over the country and to other countries too.

The majority of the employees here have worked for Miles Tea for years. We're all locals. It tends to be very gossipy! It's really nice working with people that you get along with. Of course there are ups and downs as there are anyplace, but it's an easy place to work. Some employees ride their bicycles here, which is fun in the summer and very convenient. We have a very good boss, Derek Miles. He's marvelous to work with, the ultimate English gentleman, very courteous and very charming. He's a people person. As long as you're happy and the job get's done, that's fine. Derek never comes in and says, "I want this now," it's always, "When you've got a minute," and of course you do the work straightaway. He has his tea breaks with us—Derek doesn't want to miss out on the gossip, he loves it. He cares very much about his staff, and we are very loyal to this business and of course to him.

Peddling to work is fun.

Every morning we make a big pot of tea with the loose tea for our tea break. We use fresh cold water and the kettle hits a full boil, but we don't overboil the water. And of course we always warm the teapot. The most important part of our tea break is really the biscuits though! We have about forty varieties of biscuits on hand. My favourite is the Dutch shortbread, the melt-in-the-mouth type. I need a packet a day to keep me going, they're very moreish. The company spends a fortune on all our biscuits!

I am the resident tea maker here at Miles. You can always count on hearing "Is the kettle on yet, Liz?" I don't use tea bags. Is there really any difference in the taste between tea bags and loose tea? Or is it just plain snobbery that condemns the lowly tea bag and hails that only loose tea makes a really good cup of tea? After long conversations with John our tea taster, I can now clear up any of the tea bag myths. To a certain extent the general public were a little against tea bags when they were first introduced into the market but they've now become accustomed to them. Tea bags are the norm; actually seventy percent of our tea sales go to tea bags. That figure also reflects general sales in England, with a slight discrepancy in the south of the country. For some unknown reason they lean a little more toward loose tea there. On the subject of flavour, well, there really is very little difference in flavour between our tea bag tea and our loose tea. Tea bags are not the sweepings off the floor like a lot of people used to think. When we blend the tea for the tea bag we make it a little bit stronger than our loose tea and we use finer-leafed teas to help with the infusion through the paper of the bag. Each blend of ours has about fourteen or fifteen different teas in it. With our tea bags and loose tea you'd be hard pushed to tell the difference.

I think people who use loose tea enjoy the fuss and palaver that goes with making a real pot of tea, so they don't mind waiting the statutory five minutes for it to brew properly. Loose tea drinkers tend to be more particular over the quality of their tea, far more so than tea bag customers. Those people who are in a little more of a hurry and find tea bags more convenient might be more likely to make the tea quickly and not let it brew long enough. Not brewing it long enough will make a difference in the flavour of the tea, which might be the reason why some people think there is a difference between tea bags and loose tea. You should never make a single cup of tea directly in the cup with the tea bag. You should always make tea in a teapot. Tea making is really a ritual. The whole relaxing atmosphere of making a good cup of tea the old-fashioned way is all part of the experience of tea drinking. Unfortunately we are getting away from that today.

I drink more tea in the winter months, while I do my knitting on chilly nights. Knitting in the winter is a luxury really. In the summer I like to be out in the garden. I love gardening and we have huge vegetable and flower gardens. I putter about out there for hours. You can get a lot of gardening done when the sun is up so late! Sometimes I help with the haymaking or lend a hand to shift the bullocks around, and I help out at lambing time, so spring and summer evenings are quite busy. Another of my favourite treats is to get into a lovely hot bubble bath, with the door locked and the telephone off the hook, knowing that nobody's coming around all evening. Then to snuggle down with a good book. I love to read. A cup of tea and a good novel, now that's just wonderful.

The Tea Taster's Notes

Tea made with soft water will come out lighter, brighter and with more flavour. Hard water makes tea look dull. You can counteract this by buying brighter and stronger-flavoured teas. Soft water definitely gives you a better cup of tea.

If your water is full of minerals, that will affect the flavour of tea. You could use bottled spring water.

If a good-quality tea is kept in a cool, dark, dry place it will keep for eighteen months, perhaps longer. Tea is tremendous in its ability to pick up taints from foods, so keep it in an air-tight container.

It's fun to experiment and mix teas together. That's another advantage to buying loose teas. Blend just a few spoons of tea together in case you don't like it.

The most important thing is to relax and really enjoy your tea; that's part of the English tradition.

The best way to make a cup of tea, according to John Halls, one of our professional tea tasters here at D. J. Miles:

- Pour fresh water in the kettle, allowing the tap to run for a while to make sure the water is fresh. Never reheat water.

- Allow the water to reach a full strong boil, but don't allow it to boil too long as this takes out the oxygen (the water vapor absorbs the oxygen). Overboiling the water will make the tea taste flat and look cloudy.

- Teapots come in small, medium and large sizes. Use the right-sized pot for the number of cups of tea you want to make. A small is usually for two cups, medium for four and a large for six.

- Warm the teapot with some boiling water, then pour this out after a minute. A china teapot is still the best type of pot to use.

- Spoon in the tea. One rounded spoon of tea for each person served and one extra for the pot is the rule of thumb. (Traditional silver tea serving spoons tend to hold more tea than a regular teaspoon.)

- Pour the boiling water into the teapot, stir well, replace the teapot lid and let the tea brew for about five minutes (depending on the tea and your personal taste). You can use a tea cosy to help keep the pot hot.

- Sit down and relax while you wait for your tea to brew, then pour yourself a delicious cup of tea. A china cup and saucer is wonderful to use.

If you do take milk in your tea, pour that in the cup first! Lemon you add after the tea is poured into the cup.

LIZ'S SPECKLED TEA BREAD
. . .

"This is a simple recipe for a tasty tea bread. I like it because you don't have to mess about with yeast. It's really a perfect teatime loaf. If you have a big family, I double the recipe and make two loaves. All our children love this fruity treat so it doesn't stay long in the larder."

Elizabeth Brooks

1¼ cups / 175 g mixed dried fruit, washed
1¾ cups / 350 g light brown sugar
¾ cup plus 2 tablespoons / total of 220 ml cold black tea (not herbal)

3 cups / 375 g all-purpose flour, sifted
2 medium eggs, lightly beaten
¾ cup / 105 g glacé cherries, chopped
1½ teaspoons / 6 g ground mixed spice

Soak the dried fruit and brown sugar overnight in the cold tea.

The next day, preheat your oven to 325° F/160° C. Grease an 8½ by 4½ by 2 ½-inch/22 by 11 by 6-cm loaf pan and line with greaseproof paper. Add the remaining ingredients to the soaked fruit mixture. Spoon into the pan and bake 1½ hours, until a skewer comes out clean. Cool in the pan.

Serve in thick slices, buttered.

Makes one 2-pound/1-k loaf; serves 6 to 8

SUGGESTED TEAS: Mugs of Formosa Oolong. With its slightly peachy flavour, it is delicious with a hearty, fruity tea bread. It also has a low caffeine level, which makes it a nice alternative to herbal tea to drink before going to bed. In the winter try Woodsy Lapsang souchong.

LADY JANE BOLES

*I*T'S ONE OF THOSE RAINY, MISTY ENGLISH AFTERNOONS THAT make you thankful for Wellington boots, a dependable fire in the hearth and cups of steaming hot tea. Lady Jane Boles welcomes me into her warm kitchen after a friendly greeting by Sam the Alsatian—master of the boot room. The damp coats are hung, places to sit at the pine kitchen table are established and the kettle is put on the old Aga cooker. Lady Boles pops into her larder, reappearing momentarily with an enormous chocolate cake and cups and saucers balanced pre-cariously on a tea tray. The view from the large kitchen window is expansive: rolling green hills kiss the grey skyline and are dotted with little white patches of wool. Geraniums in terra-cotta flower pots sit on the windowsill. The old pine furniture is solidly comfortable and reas-

"With the kennel there are always people popping in and out all day. Sometimes they stop for a cup of tea, which sort of delays things. But it's abso-lutely marvelous!"

suring. But what makes this room so special are the animals. A black cat named Zebadee flirts outrageously. An ancient-looking little dog peeks out from behind the leg of the over-stuffed armchair, which is occupied by another dog, a little fellow named Boots. A canary is busily preening its golden feathers in a cage by the Welsh dresser. This is an English country kitchen. Paradise Farm is a hive of activity, and when Lady Boles isn't busy making tea and serving homemade cake to the occasional visitor, she's running her dog boarding kennels, riding her horses, walking numerous canines, feeding the goats or rounding up errant chickens.

Just out!

BEING A LADYSHIP IN ENGLAND IS NOT terribly important, there are very few official functions or anything like that. Once in a while you are asked to open a country fair or present prizes and I have done my share of that sort of thing. I don't think most English people take a lot of notice of titles. It certainly doesn't mean anything in particular to me. I just happened to marry a Sir, and when you marry a Sir, you automatically become a Lady.

This farm originally belonged to my ex-husband's side of the family. The house had to be gutted and rebuilt. Where I've got my dog kennels in the yard used to be cow stalls. They converted very well because the stone buildings are cool in the summer and warm in the winter. Such lovely old buildings, just absolutely ideal for dogs. There are twenty acres all around, five fields and the hill at the back.

I can't easily keep a vegetable garden here because of the deer. They will eat anything and everything, which is why I've got my roses in tubs in the courtyard. If they were out in the garden the deer would eat them, they love roses. I've counted as many as thirty hinds in the front of the garden; they visit every night. It's lovely to see them but they are very destructive.

I have quite a selection of animals here—my horses, the goats, a turkey called Henry and his wife Henrietta—they have babies at the moment. There's various bits and pieces of poultry and four cats. The chickens don't like this rain, nor do the goats. If I leave the goats out and there's a spot of rain they make the most terrible row until I get them inside! They just hate rain. Apparently they do get pneumonia if they get wet on their backs, so they shouldn't be out in bad weather. I have six dogs of my own, an Alsatian, two terriers, two sheep dogs and a Lercher cross—a good family.

I take in about twelve dogs on the average for boarding. Each dog has its own kennel and run. They have to be exercised daily, fed and groomed. I walk them in the fields. Quite a few boarding kennels don't actually bother much about walks, but I think it's important. If you've got a dog in for several weeks, they must get exercise. I've just had a big pen put up, so that if I've got young dogs—and I very often do—I can have a game with them in there.

I opened the kennels in the autumn of 1989, but I've always had to do with dogs. I've had lots of dogs myself, as many as nine at one time. If people know you have a soft spot for dogs you always end up with the ones that people don't want. I wouldn't be without them. I do think you can go a bit silly and have too many, but having other people's dogs and making some money out of it is the next best thing to having more myself! And I have some very nice dogs in board.

My day starts just before seven, first letting the house dogs out. I love reading so I usually make myself a cup of tea and go back to bed and read for a while. Then I get up and I let the poultry out—they're free-range and peck about all over the farm—and I check on the horses in the fields. After that the kennel dogs go out in turn, and I clean out their runs. Each one gets a biscuit and usually they settle back on their beds. I have another cup of tea and perhaps cereal or a bit of fruit before I start walking the dogs, which takes quite a while because I give each of them a good walk. You get masses of exercise running a kennel. Sometimes I take two or three at a time, if they're nice dogs, you know, and get on well together. If one's a little aggressive then I take it out on its own. My own big dogs go out with me when I ride. I don't take the two little ones, they can't keep up, but the four big dogs do fine with the horse. We go up over the hill through the fields. It's lovely. In the afternoon there's a bit of a gap so I might do some shopping or something in town.

I start work again with the late afternoon feeding, but that depends on the weather. If it's a very hot day I don't feed the dogs too early because I don't think it's good for them. So I might be a bit later

A dear friend.

but generally about four o'clock I start letting them out in the yard in turn, and getting their evening meals. After clearing up all their bowls and things, it's often half-past seven or eight before I finish washing up. I don't watch much television, but I do like to see the news once a day, so I very often catch the nine o'clock news while I have a bit of supper. Before you know it the day is gone. I always read in bed before I sleep and sometimes I'll have a cup of herb tea, it's very relaxing.

I've got quite a few friends in the area and I often go out for supper or somebody comes here. With the kennels there are always people popping in and out all day. Sometimes they stop for a cup of tea, which sort of delays things. But it's absolutely marvelous! My regular tea is P.G. Tips. I don't actually like China tea or Earl Grey.

A scrumptious teatime treat.

As I said, I do drink herbal tea in the evenings but never at teatime. It would be very rare for me to have an actual formal tea party. But quite often a friend will drop in about teatime and we have a cup of tea and a bit of cake. If I know they're dropping in I might make a chocolate cake. I've usually got a fruitcake on the go—they're a good standby. When it's getting near the end I make another one, so I always have one on hand.

For me, afternoon tea is sitting down for five minutes! You can't gallop around working. That's really what tea is, having a break. If I'm here on my own I still have tea and perhaps read the paper or pick up my book. When the children were living at home, we didn't always have tea together. It was pretty much help yourself at mealtimes, except for suppertime. I've always been working and the children were all going off in different directions. Come to think of it, I don't recall that we've ever had a sit-down breakfast together, I don't think so! Each one of us got what we wanted ourselves. Even from a very young age all my children could cook. If they came home and I was out, they always knew how to get themselves their tea. If all the family were here, we would have a cup of tea and a biscuit or a slice of cake together. Tea would be a time for being together.

Before I inherited the farm, I worked in Bristol. I was divorced and a single mother of three, which was a big undertaking but I couldn't live with my husband any longer. Being single was better than that. I thrive on hard work, I really work much better when I'm under pressure and there's not enough time to do things. My biggest challenge was keeping a home going that the children could bring their friends to and just making sure the whole thing was flowing. It wasn't easy because I was at the office all day and then after work I'd dash off to do the shopping on the way home and then cook an evening meal. It was quite hectic. The weekends were spent washing and ironing, cleaning the house, cooking and preparing for the following week. That was my life, just keeping the whole thing going. It was worth it. Stability is so important for children.

Then my aunt-in-law, Aunt Nesta, who lived here, was in a very bad car accident. She went into a coma for about four months, then died. I found she had left me this property. That was the beginning of the really hard work. She had lived here for twenty years and had owned it for forty, but didn't bother much with it. It was in a dreadful state, the ceilings had fallen down, the walls were crumbling, there was very little electricity and what there was wasn't really working, and no heating of any kind. The main part of the house is at least four to five hundred years old.

Inheriting her home was a horror! Besides it being a very sad time, there was such a lot to do; her companion was bedridden, I had race horses here that needed looking after and the electric plugs got burning hot if you used them. It was all very primitive. I slept for three months in the little sitting room with the fire going. I had to keep getting up in the middle of the night to put logs on the fire because it was freezing in the house. There wasn't a bedroom to sleep in at all and it was a particularly cold winter that year.

It was very spooky here, the farm wasn't a bit like it is now. There were bushes all around, it was terribly overgrown and someone had put newspapers up in all the windows blocking out any trace of light, the house was overgrown, dark, cold and really quite frightening. I borrowed my son's Alsatian dog and I felt much better then.

I suppose it was rather unusual to inherit from my ex-husband's aunt, but Aunt Nesta was very fond of me and she knew I would look after this place and love it. And she wanted my children to have it because she knew they would love it too. Paradise Farm absolutely changed my life. I'm terribly grateful to Aunt Nesta. Instead of living in Bristol and having to work from nine to five in an office, I now have enormous freedom. I think that's what I'm most grateful for—my freedom. I sold up my house in Bristol and put quite a bit of that money into this place. Doing it up and being able to make this place work and getting a living out of it has made me quite independent. I was absolutely determined when I completed the remodeling that I

wanted to work here and I knew there was a great need for a kennel in the area. I've got a small private income but really the dog boarding has doubled my monthly receipts. I opened the kennels in October and was full in November. I never believed it would take on like that, but all the veterinary practises in the area send their clients here.

I've got a lot of friends and if I do feel a bit fed up with my own company, I ring somebody up and say, "Come and have some supper," or, "Stop in for a cup of tea." I know myself well enough that if I have a lot of evenings, especially in the winter, all on my own, then I do get a bit low. I know I do, so I sort of work accordingly.

I am extremely fortunate to have such wonderful children, all my lovely dogs and animals and this farm. It's been very hard work, sometimes I wonder how I got through a few of the rough spots, but you just carry on, work a bit harder and sooner or later things always sort themselves out. This place really *is* a Paradise for me. Would you like another cup of tea before I go out to the kennels?

LADY JANE BOLES'
CHOCOLATE SPONGE
· · ·

"This is a rather naughty cake, it's very chocolatey and decadent. My children and grandchildren love it, consequently it doesn't stay in the cake tin very long. Besides being excellent for afternoon tea, it's a fabulous dessert for a dinner party. You can serve fresh raspberries with it, which is delicious, and perhaps a dollop of whipped cream too, if you're being terribly naughty!"

Jane Boles

FOR THE SPONGE CAKE
2 cups/250 g all-purpose flour
1/2 cup/100 g cocoa powder
1 teaspoon/4 g baking soda
1/4 teaspoon/1 g salt
1 1/4 cups/250 g superfine white sugar
1/2 cup/125 g softened margarine
2 large eggs
1/4 cup/60 ml whole milk

FOR THE ICING
3/4 cup/150 g powdered sugar
1/8 cup/24 g cocoa powder
1/4 cup/60 g butter
1/4 cup/50 g superfine white sugar
2 tablespoons/30 ml water

To make the cake: Preheat your oven to 350° F/175° C. Grease two 7-inch/18-cm cake pans.

Sift the flour, cocoa, baking soda and salt together into a medium-sized bowl. With a wooden spoon, mix in the sugar and margarine. Beat the eggs and milk with a fork in a small bowl and add to the sugar mixture. Mix all ingredients carefully and beat until light and fluffy. Pour the batter into the pans and bake approximately 30 minutes. Cool in the pans for 5 minutes, then turn out on wire racks and cool completely before spreading the filling and icing the top of the cake.

To make the icing: Sift the powdered sugar and cocoa into a small bowl. Put the butter, sugar and water in a saucepan and stir over low heat until the butter is melted and the sugar is dissolved. Bring to a boil and pour into the dry ingredients. Beat well with a spoon. Leave to set, stirring occasionally until thickened.

Spread icing on one of the cakes, then sandwich the cakes together. (You can replace the icing filling with raspberry jam for a less sweet cake.) Spread the remaining icing over the top of the cake. Decorate each serving with fresh raspberries (if in season) and a washed green nonpoisonous leaf.

Makes one 7-inch/18-cm double cake; serves 12

SUGGESTED TEAS: Serve with good full-bodied Assam tea, or an Oolong from Formosa. A raspberry-flavoured black tea or a raspberry-herbal tea would be delicious with this chocolate cake also.

The Great British Cuppa

Assam tea from India is one of the boldest of teas, with high colour and a strong, bright flavour. Blended Assam is an English favourite. This great British cuppa is commonly enjoyed with milk and perhaps sugar. The addition of sugar does diffuse the flavour of the tea, but many English people have a sweet tooth and insist on their cuppa being sweetened, sometimes with as many as five heaped teaspoons for a single cup! Assam with lemon is not as complementary to the chocolate cake. If you are a newcomer to tea, try your Assam with just a small splash of milk and no sweetener.

FRANCES EDWARDS

Driving west from Wimbelball Lake along the narrow road banked by high hedgerows, you will find Pulhams Mill at the bottom of the hill. It is a beautiful old stone flour mill newly converted into an artists' workshop and craft boutique. The courtyard displays handcrafted garden benches and picnic tables; the showroom is filled with the works of local artists—paintings of delicate wildflowers and country scenes, furniture, teapot trivets, hand-painted china and all manner of handcrafted items. I was on a last-minute mission to buy a wedding present when I was distracted by a splendidly carved rocking horse in the corner. Sitting on the horse's back were three absolutely gorgeous teddy bears. Pulhams Mill is the only craft studio in England that sells Frankie's bears. A week later I met Frankie Edwards at an antiques and crafts fair held at the Carnarvon Arms, a rambling country hotel near the beautiful West Somerset country town of Dulverton. Frankie stood at the front of the room, behind a large table covered with adorable bears. Appropriate introductions were made to all the teddies: Archie, Boris, Bertie, Toby, Sara, Willum and Oscar. Not only did Lord Liscombe, an extremely handsome bear, come home with me, but Frankie also invited us both to a teddy bears' tea party the following week.

"I love a real sit-down tea. You don't have traditional teas so much these days in England. Honey on bread and butter is all very well for bears, but what I adore is a cup of tea with a cream cake."

Adorable Edwards Bears.

DO YOU KNOW THAT A FAVOURITE TEATIME TREAT for teddy bears is brown bread and butter with lashings of honey? Bears simply adore honey, but watch out for sticky paws and messy noses! Teddies can get into a terrible mess with honey. And they drink gallons of tea, so you must keep the kettle going all the time at a teddy tea party—it's essential.

Everyone knows I'm quite crazy about bears. My children, Leeann and Stephen, are just as bad as me. They send me teddy cards, teddy ornaments, anything with a teddy on it. We have teddies all over the house now. Every time I go to see the children I take them a bear each. Leeann and Stephen have got masses of them.

Stephen is a partner in a nursing home in Tunbridge Wells, a lovely place. One bear went up to visit and the elderly people loved him, so I took more up on my next visit and now they all have their own teddies. They find them a tremendous comfort. There's a big bear called George who sits in their sitting room. Bless them, everyone says "Good morning" to George before going into breakfast.

My bears are really a hobby-cum-business. I had always made soft toys for the children when they were small and then a couple of years ago I started making bears. The first lot I made sold so easily. Someone would buy a bear and their friends would admire it and before you know it I'd receive a check in the post with a note saying they saw so-and-so's bear and could they order one too. Each batch I made after that just got better and better looking. I have customers from all over England now and abroad. I've sent bears to Manhattan, Canada, New Zealand, Italy, Paris and Zimbabwe. They keep me very busy. Some days it's difficult for me to squeeze in a cup of tea, let alone a tea party!

I love a real sit-down tea. You don't have traditional teas so much these days in England. Honey on bread and butter is all very well for bears, but what I adore is a cup of tea with a cream cake. To be invited by an old friend for tea is lovely. I've got some wonderful young-at-heart friends who have incredible teas. One dear friend serves a delicious herbal tea with flowers floating in the cup. A couple of my friends come from very wealthy families where they had the nursery tea as children, so they really know how to have a proper afternoon tea. The table is always set with a white linen and lace tablecloth, tea is served in the best English bone china and the crustless cucumber sandwiches are so delicate you can eat masses of them.

When I go up and visit Mum we always have tea together. My favourite cream cakes usually appear, which is a spoiler. When I was a child Mum always worked, so her mother had a big part in bringing us up. As a child, it was always tea with Nan. We had sweet things, no savories at all. I loved the sugar sandwiches—thin white bread spread with butter, then sugar sprinkled on. On Sundays we had a traditional Sunday roast lunch at twelve and then our tea with Mum at four

Frankie's favourite—a birthday cream cake.

o'clock. I remember one teatime when Mum caught the cat dipping its paw in the milk jelly bowl. She was fit to be tied. (We heard her shouting at the cat in the kitchen. "Just wipe it off Mum," we yelled to her, but we were too late. She flung it down the loo. The jelly, not the cat!)

I suppose we are a tea type of family really. My son takes his fiancée to the Ritz for tea. Of course she loves that. He took me to a lovely tea shop in Tunbridge Wells last year. The old-fashioned maids came up and served us in their pinafores and mobcaps and they had a trolley full of fantastic cakes. Usually we are all buzzing around and far too busy to stop, so to go out for tea and relax is a lovely change.

Here at home I usually just grab a mug of tea around three o'clock; sometimes I have a biscuit with it. I love mashed-up bananas on toast and hot buttered crumpets too. I usually drink my tea as I stitch up a bear. It's sip and stitch, sip and stitch. I can make an average-sized bear of nineteen inches in a day. I get all the cutouts done and bagged up and then I start sewing. My goal is to make a bear a day. I like to see a new face daily. I always hand-stitch first to get a good shape, then machine-sew. All my bears have happy faces, smiling mouths. It's taken me two years to crack the smile correctly, to get the faces, noses and mouths how I really want them. I don't like downturned faces.

Once a month I try to do a big country fair. Stratford-upon-Avon had an interesting bear fair last month which every teddy lover would have enjoyed. I was amazed when I arrived. There were just thousands and thousands of bears—different shapes and sizes, old and young, it was wonderful! The characters I met! And the lovely people. Young men and their wives carrying their beautiful great bears around. They brought them to see the other bears, you see. Teddy bear lovers are quite fanatic, you know. Some people had their teddies tucked in their coats, so teddy could see out. I met a couple who were enjoying afternoon tea and their bear sat with them. Yes, he had his own chair and his own cup and saucer. It was marvelous!

I had to make twin bears for twin boys a few months ago. I cut the teddies out on the day the twins were born, so they would have the same birthdays. I made them two huge, hairy brown bears. I tried to make them as identical as possible but I did give them different coloured eyes so the boys wouldn't fight over whose was whose. That sort of order is great fun and always a pleasure to make up.

One of my bears has a home with a Romanian girl. She was rescued from Romania when Ceausescu was in power. They had to smuggle her out. She was absolutely overwhelmed when I gave it to her; she adored him. She had never had a bear. I don't think she had ever had any toys at all. She went to her new home with her bear in a little bag. Bears don't like being wrapped up. They go off in a bag with their head sticking out, so they can see.

I'm fussy where they go, mind you. I was at a show once and someone was muttering something about buying a bear for their dog. I wouldn't sell them one, because I should have thought the dog would have ripped it up. I like my bears to go to good homes. Generally, nice people buy bears—mainly adults, who buy them as gifts or for themselves. Surprisingly, I sell far many more teddy bears for adults than for children.

I don't want my bear-making hobby to get really big, because I don't want to ask anybody else to help me other than my mum. I like designing my own patterns and any teddy that's not quite saleable I just put aside until a friend stops by with a child in tow. If a bear has got a crooked eye or a funny nose it doesn't matter to a child. So the rejects go upstairs in the baby crib until they are given away to friends.

I like the independence I have with my hobby-cum-business— my teddies. My world has turned upside down in the last few years, what with one thing and another. I now drive all over England to teddy fairs. I meet fabulous people. I would never have dreamt that things would have turned out like this. But I can't imagine my life without my children and my bears— and the occasional good strong cup of tea to keep me going!

Old friends—worn and loved.

Crumpet Notes

Since crumpet rings are hard to find, use 3- or 4-inch egg-frying rings—they work beautifully. Tuna fish cans with tops and bottoms removed work well also.

Making crumpets might seem a bit of a bother, with all that setting-aside and warming, but it's well worth the time and effort. Homemade crumpets are out of this world, but you should *never* eat cold crumpets, always toast them first. You can use a toasting fork to toast your crumpets in front of the fire. Toast the smooth side first, then the holey side; this way, when you butter the holey side, it's hottest and will have slight indentations for the butter to melt into (crumpet etiquette of the best order) or simply pop in the toaster. Crumpets are usually considered a wintertime afternoon tea treat. You would not see crumpets served in the spring or summer months in England—absolutely not!

"I can remember having toasted crumpets dripping with butter when I was a child. They are lovely on a cold winter's day. Enjoy them with a strong cup of tea in front of the fire. Toast them well and serve them hot with butter and jam."

Frances Edwards

3 cups/375 g unbleached
    all-purpose flour
2 teaspoons/8 g salt
1¼ cups/310 ml whole milk
    mixed with 1¼ cups/
    310 ml water

2 tablespoons/30 ml
    vegetable oil
¾ teaspoon/3 g sugar
2 teaspoons/8 g active dry
    yeast
½ teaspoon/2 g baking soda
Warm water

Sift the flour and salt into a mixing bowl and warm in a low oven for 15 minutes. In a medium-sized saucepan, warm the milk and water with the oil and sugar. Stir in the dry yeast and leave in a warm place until frothy.

Make a well in the center of the warmed flour mixture. Pour in the yeast mixture, stir and beat hard for 5 minutes with a fork or whisk (you want it very airy). Cover the bowl with a clean cloth and leave for 2 hours at room temperature (the surface should be covered with bubbles).

Dissolve the baking soda in 2 to 3 tablespoons/30 to 45ml warm water in a measuring cup. Stir into the batter and beat for 2 minutes more. Cover the bowl again and let stand 1 hour.

Lightly grease your crumpet rings and a large, heavy frying pan or griddle (you can use a nonstick spray). Heat the griddle to medium-hot, place 3 or 4 rings on it at a time, and fill each ring almost to the top with the batter. Heat gently until the surface is full of holes. (If holes do not appear, the batter may be too thick; add a little warm water to your next batch.) Remove the rings, turn the crumpets and cook an additional 4 minutes. Butter and serve immediately, plain or with jam. They can be served later after toasting on both sides.

Makes 8 to 10 crumpets

SUGGESTED TEAS: If you top your crumpets with black currant jam, try a black currant tea. An Irish breakfast tea (Assam and Ceylon blend) is strong and hearty and very good with milk and sugar (if you like sweetened tea). This is an excellent tea to enjoy with mouthwatering, buttered crumpets.

$\mathscr{T}$HE ENGLISH TEA TRADITION MAY BE LOST WITH THE NEXT generation. In this final conversation two young English women, Emma and Helen, both fifteen years old, share their thoughts with us. Coming from two very different backgrounds, Emma and Helen are united in their friendship—over a cup of tea on a sunny afternoon in the garden. Emma's life is somewhat affluent; she has a beautiful horse and a pedigree dog and lives in a large country home in a secluded setting with acres of grounds to explore. Emma's mother, secretary to the West Somerset Hunt Pony Club, is active in many charitable organizations, works with investment property, assists her husband in his business and is a homemaker. Emma's father is an international solicitor and property investor. Helen's lifestyle is humbler. She lives in the town in a simple yet comfortable semidetached brick house with a small garden. The house is located on a busy road in a modest neighbourhood. Her mother is a homemaker and her father is a policeman in the town. While Emma attends many of her parents' social functions, enters horse shows and plays cricket, Helen's focus is on her schoolwork and spending time with her two younger sisters. Afternoon tea, for both these young ladies, is not a featured family gathering time. Which leads to the question . . . Is afternoon tea a disappearing English tradition?

"I thought the tradition of afternoon tea had really died out, something that was an old-fashioned thing to do. I hadn't realized how often we actually have tea until we started talking about it." (Emma, left and Helen, right)

A classic English afternoon tea celebration.

EMMA: WHEN I COME home from school and have something to eat, that's what I think of as teatime. I'll make a cup of tea unless it's very hot, then I'll have a milkshake. We don't drink much iced tea in England. I usually head straight for the biscuits—the chocolate digestives. If we have some cake I might have a piece of that. My mother doesn't like making cakes so I started to make them and I've gone on from there. I quite often make a lemon cake so I might have a slice or two of that, it's very lemony and really yummy. This is not what is called a proper English afternoon tea. We don't have that in our home.

My younger brother Alexander is twelve. He usually comes home from school and watches television while he has a cup of tea and something to eat. I'll have my tea in the kitchen, but on nice days I sometimes go out in the garden. Tea in our house is not really a family thing. Sometimes in the summer we'll all have tea outside together, or we might take tea and biscuits on a tray into the sitting room. That's very unusual though. It's nothing grand, like you see in the old films. Helen, when I asked you to come over to tea what did you think?

Helen: I didn't know what you meant, Emma. I wasn't sure if I was being invited for a cup of tea or a real tea. When I come home from school I don't usually have tea—just an orange juice and a packet of crisps while I'm watching the telly. When relatives come for a visit we often go for a walk and then we might go out for tea.

We like The Tea Shoppe in Dunster, it's a fifteenth-century cottage restaurant. Pam and Norman Goldsack are the owners. Pam makes fabulous scones and cakes, she's a really great cook and has won quite a few awards.

Sometimes I'll make a cake and then we might have tea outside if the weather's nice; that's quite rare though, too. My mum taught me to make cakes when I was younger. We don't usually sit down for tea and cake. You just grab a slice when you want it in our house, we don't have a formal tea thing—ever. I really like drinking tea at dinnertime and late at night—it helps to keep me going, to get my homework done.

Emma: Helen's a good student, she gets all her schoolwork in on time. I'm not so good. On nice evenings I'd much rather ride my horse. I'm in the Pony Club and you have to ride several times a week to keep your horse in fit condition. My horse is called Snoopy, he's lovely, he's fifteen hands. We do all the local shows and gymkhanas together.

Fiona serving tea at The Tea Shoppe in Dunster.

I like most sports, all the games. Sometimes I get to play cricket on my father's team, which is fun. Once in a while we have tea and cucumber sandwiches in the pavilion after the match. On hot days some spectators bring hampers and have tea on the green while they watch the cricket. If it's raining they all stay in their cars or huddle under umbrellas shivering. I suppose hot tea is great then too.

Helen: I play hockey and net ball but Emma is really the athlete. I like going to discos.

Emma: Discos are fun. Nobody would be seen dead drinking tea there though. We have cokes.

Helen: What's the most exciting thing that's ever happened to you, Emma?

Emma: Oh my god! Do you want the truth? Oh, crumbs! I suppose it's liking a certain boy.

Helen: Oh yes, dating.

Emma: Dating? Well it's sort of dating, nobody has a car. Usually my parents drop me off at the pictures or sometimes boys come up to the house for dinner with the family. Not often though. It's really exciting when a boy you like, likes you.

Helen: I've been to tea at my boyfriend's parents' house.

Emma: For tea! You had tea with him?

Helen: Yes, we had sandwiches, cake, biscuits and tea. It wasn't a big formal thing. It was fun, I was a bit nervous. Dating a boy is unusual for me. I have to get home quite early on school nights. Occasionally I'm allowed to go to a friend's house to do my homework, watch a video and then come home. We often have mugs of tea to help us keep awake. If it's a weekend and there's a party I usually stay at somebody's house nearby.

Emma: Those parties are the best fun. I like staying the night at someone's house. It's great having a party as long as it isn't held in your own house.

Helen: It's too much hassle if it's your own house.

Emma: I have quite a few Pony Club events to go to on the weekends and I have to get up early to get my horse ready. I don't think I've ever missed a party, but sometimes I'm a bit whacked out because I haven't had enough sleep the night before!

It takes quite a long time to get a horse ready for a show. Washing, grooming, trimming and plaiting up the mane takes ages, but horses really look smart when it's done well. All the tack has to be spotless and polished; cleaning a saddle can take forever. And then getting into your gear— Mum is really great about getting all my riding clothes together, shirt ironed and all that stuff.

Helen: Emma helps the younger riders a lot too. Some have to go on the leading rein and be led around the jumping course. It's fun to watch them. Some of the girls are so tiny they sort of balance and bobble around on the saddle,

Gymkhanas are English field days held for junior equestrians.

their legs are barely long enough for the stirrups. Usually they only go over very low jumps. They look really sweet in their jodhpurs, boots and riding hats.

Emma: Last year at Pony Club camp we had a fabulous tea. All week we have riding instruction and jumping practise, then the last day is a day of events. Parents and friends come and watch us as we compete against each other. At the end of the day there's this huge presentation—certifications, rosettes, even cups are awarded sometimes. This is when all the thank-you's are said, all that type of thing. Then there's a huge tea, which is usually set up in a barn or out on the lawn if the weather's nice. All the mums bring sandwiches—egg and cress, meat paste, ham and sausage rolls, crisps, cakes and biscuits. The little ones have orange squash and there's masses of tea in huge tea urns for everyone else. We go through gallons of the stuff.

Helen: I like going to the big county shows with my friend Jenny. Her dad is a farmer. At these shows there are hundreds of farm animals competing for champion of the county—best ram, best sow with piglets, best cow, bull, chickens, all that sort of thing. If you're a member of the Country Landowners' Association you can go into their huge Members Only tent. They serve lunch and afternoon tea and glasses of champagne and have flowers all over the place. It's expensive but very nice if you like that sort of thing. You can also get tea from the exhibitors, like the tractor and farm equipment manufacturers. They have sandwiches and biscuits laid out in their display tents. If your parents are farmers you can go in and look at the tractors and they offer you tea.

Emma: I like the smaller shows and gymkhanas, they have good teas there too and there's always a cake contest. After the judging, the cakes all get auctioned off. Some ladies are known for being brilliant cooks, so their cakes always go for the highest prices. You can buy tea and slices of cake at gymkhanas but its more fun to bid on a cake and take it back to the horse-jumping ring and watch the events while you sit on a blanket and scoff it! We take a thermos of

We don't drink much iced tea in England.

tea and sometimes the adults have G and T's [gin and tonics]. My parents' friends come by and it turns into a car boot picnic. Most of the time I'm off riding in one of the events but I usually get a slice of cake and a cup of tea saved for me.

Helen: We have tea at school functions too. Parents' Day and Prize Day—it's quite usual to have tea then. All the mums get rung up beforehand and are talked into bringing a plate of sandwiches, a jam sponge or a fruitcake. Jenny's mum always makes a brilliant coffee cake—it's fabulous and has loads of thick, creamy coffee icing.

I thought the tradition of afternoon tea had really died out, something that was an old-fashioned thing to do. I hadn't realized how often we actually have tea until we started talking about it. It's true, we may not have a proper tea at home, but we have tea at a lot of other times in England.

Emma: I think the Americans and Australians think English girls are old-fashioned, that we are a bit behind with our private schools and uniforms and afternoon tea and all of that. We aren't really old-fashioned.

Helen: England isn't like it used to be. Life isn't like what you see in the old films. We don't all sit down to afternoon tea at four o'clock in our best frocks. Most people don't have silver teapots and posh, fancy things. Those films make us look old-fashioned and like fuddy-duddies, but we aren't. It's true that we do drink a lot more tea in England, perhaps more than in other places in the world, but that doesn't make us different from anyone else. We're not really different at all. We are English and we just drink tea.

EMMA'S FAMOUS LEMON CAKE

· · ·

"I often make this cake when I come home from school. It's awfully quick and easy. Mum and Dad like it, so does my brother, it's just terrific. If a friend comes over we can scoff practically the whole cake, so be warned it's addictive! Use mugs if it's just a casual tea for chums. If Grandmother or somebody important is coming, use the best china cups and saucers!"

Emma Maitland-Walker

1 cup/250 g softened
    margarine
1 cup/200 g superfine
    white sugar
3 large eggs
    (free-range if possible)

2 cups/250 g all-purpose flour
⅓ cup/80 ml freshly squeezed
    lemon juice and grated rind
    of 1 large lemon (only
    yellow zest, not white pith)

Preheat your oven to 350° F/175° C. Grease a 5 by 9-inch/13 by 23-cm loaf pan.

In a medium-sized bowl, cream the margarine and sugar together until light and fluffy (use a wooden spoon or a mixer). Add the eggs and flour and whisk together. Add the lemon juice and grated rind and whisk again. Pour the batter into the pan and bake 30 to 35 minutes. Cool in the pan for 5 minutes, then turn out onto a rack to cool. Cut into ¾-inch/2-cm slices.

Serves up to 12, or 2 hungry teenagers

SUGGESTED TEAS: Earl Grey tea or herbal lemon (hot or iced) are yummy. Iced tea is wonderful on a hot summer afternoon. It's fun to freeze lemon slices or mint leaves in ice cubes; they look beautiful in a long tall glass and add an extra zip of flavour to the tea. Leftover tea? Freeze it! Make into ice cubes.

The Popular Earl Grey

Earl Grey tea is named after the second Earl Grey, who brought it back from China in 1830. Made from large-leafed China tea blended with Darjeeling and scented with oil of bergamot, it has a fine delicate flavour and is delicious with cakes. Be careful: some brands of Earl Grey tend to overdo the oil and it is then very perfumey. Brands can vary greatly, try a few to see which one suits your taste best.

DIRECTORY

Some helpful names and addresses should you plan a visit to England.

Hindon Farm 0643-705244
Nr. Minehead
Somerset TA24 8SH
England
Hosts: Penny and Roger Webber
Farmhouse Bed-and-Breakfast
(Reservations a must; write for a
brochure)

Edwards Bears 0502-724054
Frankie Edwards

Periwinkle Cottage 0643-862769
Selworthy
Nr. Minehead
Somerset TA24 8TP
England
Hosts: Chris and Mike Taylor
Afternoon teas/lunches
(Open from March to October; closed
on Mondays)

The Tea Shoppe 0643-821304
3 High Street
Dunster
Somerset TA24 6SS
England
Hosts: Pamela and Norman Goldsack
Afternoon teas/lunches/dinner
(Open seven days a week from March
to end of October; November and
December open on weekends only)

Pulhams Mill Studio 03987-366
Brompton Regis
Nr. Dulverton
Somerset TA22 9NT
England
Host: Pauline Clements
Art/crafts and furniture
(Open all year, except for Christmas
and following week)

Fortnum and Mason 071-7348040
181 Piccadilly
London W1AIER
England
Tea suppliers; St. James Restaurant for
afternoon tea
(Reservations recommended)

The Ritz Hotel 071-4938181
Piccadilly
London W1V9DG
England
The Palm Court for afternoon tea
(Reservations a must)

Harrods Ltd 071-7301234
Knightsbridge
London SW1
England
Specialty teas; the Georgian Restau-
rant for afternoon tea
(Reservations recommended)

Frances Fry 0643-706284
Artist
Painting and sculpture commissions

D. J. Miles & Co. 0643-862585
Vale Yard
High Street
Porlock
Somerset TA24 8PU
England
Tea and coffee merchants

The National Trust 071-2229251
36 Queen Annes Gate
London SW1 H9AS
England
Charitable trust for the preservation
of places of historic interest or natural
beauty. International membership
available and information regarding
tours of stately homes, castles, interest
points, gardens, etc.

Longleat 0985-44400
The Estate Office
Warminster
Wiltshire BA12 7NW
England
Tours of the stately home, gardens and
safari park; write for a brochure.

INDEX

Page numbers in italics refer to illustrations.